The Healing POWER OF WORDS

Dr Michael Mosesian

AUTHOR'S NOTE:

Writing this collection of poems has been both a challenge and a joy. As someone who has experienced loss in various forms, I wanted to create a collection that would offer solace, comfort, and inspiration to those who are struggling to make sense of their pain. I wanted to create a space where the nuances and complexities of grief could be explored in a way that was personal and honest.

These poems speak to universal themes of love, loss, and the human experience of suffering. While each poem is inspired by the experiences of many people, they are also the result of my own reflections on the subject. My hope is that these poems will serve as a companion to those who are facing loss, and that they will offer a way to connect with the beauty and resilience that lies within.

In writing this collection, I have been reminded once again of the healing power of words. I believe that poetry has a unique ability to give voice to the inexpressible, to capture the raw emotional power of grief, and to offer a way forward towards healing and renewal.

It is my hope that these poems will resonate with readers on a deep and personal level. That they will offer comfort, solace, and hope to those who are struggling to make sense of their pain, and that they will serve as a reminder that even in the darkest of times, there is always hope.

TABLE OF CONTENTS

Endless Chill 11
Broken Open: Finding Beauty in the Ashes of Grief 13
A Tapestry of Grief and Hope 15
Tidal Wave of Grief: Navigating Loss and Healing 17
Shattered Yet Rising 19
Hope's Flickering Flame 21
When Hope Bursts Forth 23
Flames of Hope: Igniting the Path to a Better Future 25
Healing: A Journey of Light and Shadow 27
Clutches of Sorrow: A Journey to Hope 29
Journey to Healing: A Transformational Process 31
Echoes of Loss: Honouring Memories and Finding Strength 33
Unyielding Strength: The Fire Within 35
Adaptation: The Dance with Fate 37
Shattered Reflections: A Poetic Odyssey of Loss and Resilience 39
Resilience: A Journey of the Human Spirit 41
Echoes of Sorrow: A Journey Through Grief 43
Resilience: A Poem of Triumph 45
Dance of Resilience: The Symphony of Strength 47
Unbreakable: The Resilient Heart 49
Whispers of Absence 51
Love Endures Beyond Loss 53
Love Still Present Despite Loss 55
Eternal Flame: Love that Endures Beyond Loss 57
Ghosts of Love 59
Love Endures 61
Eternal Bond 63
Forever in My Heart 65
Last Embrace: A Poem of Farewell and Hope 67
Love's Legacy: Finding Peace After Loss 69

Eternal Light: A Tribute to My Grandmother 71
The Eternal Flame of Love 73
Eternal Foundations: Love Beyond Death 75
Rising Strong: Poetry of Perseverance and Courage 77
Letting Go 79
Echoes of Departure 81
Absence of a Guiding Light 83
A Mother's Light 85
The Ever-Evolving Dance of Life 87
The Lasting Presence of Grandfather 89
A Mother's Reflections on Loss 91
The Weight of Brother's Loss 93
Last Embrace: A Bittersweet Goodbye 95
Conquering the Shadow 97
Resilience Amidst Tragedy 99
The Weight of War 101
Tender Tears: A Poem of Love and Loss for Mourning Parents 103
Echoes of a Mourning Soulmate 105
Forever in My Heart: A Poem on the Unforgettable Love of a Mother . .107
Sudden Passing 109
Memories that Endure 111
Fading Light: A Poem on the Worsening Health of a Loved One 113
Haunting Shadows: A Journey Through Trauma 115
Echoes of Solitude: Grieving the Loss of Love 117
Love Beyond the Veil 119
Mourning's Embrace 121
Whispers in the Wind: A Poem on Love and Loss 123
Unbreakable Love: A Song Beyond Death 125
Echoes of Everlasting Love: A Song of the Undying Bond 127
Strength in Grief: A Journey of Resilience and Hope 129
Journey Through Mourning: Finding Myself in the Depths of Sorrow . .131
When Grief Becomes a Strength: The Power of Resilience 133

Whispers in the Wind: Remembering My Grandfather 135
Echoes of Love: A Poem of Grief and Remembrance for My Grandma.. 137
From Darkness to Light: A Poem of Loss and Triumph 139
A Poetic Journey of Resilience 141
Unbreakable Flame: The Strength Within.......................... 143
Unwavering Strength... 145
Hope's Eternal Flame 147
Support 149
Embracing the Dance of Change................................... 151
Believing in Oneself.. 153
Reaching Out: A Journey of Vulnerability and Strength 155
Overcoming Loss with Resilience and Strength 157
Whispers of the Wind: A Journey of Loss and Resilience Through the Ebb and Flow of Life's Tides 159
Unbreakable Shards... 161
The Roots of Strength 163
The Light Within... 165
Eternal Flames of Love 167
The Healing Power of Collective Grief: Finding Strength in Community 169
Nature's Embrace: A Balm for the Grieving Heart.................. 171
New Beginning: A Journey Through Grief and Healing 173
Creative Healing... 175
Threads of Memory: Weaving Resilience in the Face of Loss 177
Grateful Resilience: The Power of Self-Appreciation in the Face of Loss. 179
Love's Healing Power 181
Unveiling the Power of Self-Care: A Journey Towards Resilience and Healing 183
Finding Light in the Dark: The Healing Power of Laughter 185
Legacy: The Everlasting Light 187
The Art of Letting Go.. 189
Finding Strength in Music's Embrace............................. 191
The Transformative Power of Travel.............................. 193

The Transformative Power of Pets in Times of Sorrow and Healing.....195
Traditions, the Keepers of Hope 197
Bonds of Friendship 199
Finding Strength in Helping Others................................201
The Healing Power of Food 203
Penning Strength: Healing Through Writing 205
Art's Comfort: A Source of Solace in the Night 207
Overcoming Grief with the Support of Family.......................209
Resilience in Motion: The Healing Power of Sports and Physical
Activity 211
Serenity's Triumph: How Meditation Empowers Resilience and
Heals Grief 213
The Comfort of Adventure 215
The Healing Power of Kindness 217
The Guiding Light of Education....................................219
The Magic of Acceptance...221
Pixels of Solace: Technology's Role in Healing the Heart 223
Activism's Flame 225
The Healing Power of Cooking......................................227
Acknowledgments: 229
    Support services 231

PREFACE:

Loss is a universal human experience that touches each of us in different ways. Whether it is the death of a loved one, the end of a relationship, or the loss of a job or a dream, the pain and confusion that come with loss can be overwhelming. In such times, it can be difficult to find the words to express our feelings, to make sense of our pain, and to find a way forward.

This book is a collection of poems that speaks to the heart of the human experience of grief and loss. It is a testament to the power of words to heal, comfort, and inspire us in times of need. These poems explore the many dimensions of grief and loss, from the initial shock and numbness to the long process of healing and renewal. They offer a way to connect with the depths of our emotions and discover the beauty and resilience that lies within.

As a poet, I have always been drawn to the power of language to express the inexpressible. In my own experience of loss, I have found solace and healing in the words of others who have traveled a similar path. It is my hope that these poems will offer a similar sense of comfort and inspiration to those who are struggling to make sense of their pain.

I believe that poetry has a unique ability to speak to the heart of the human experience. It has the power to capture the nuances and complexities of our emotions in a way that other forms of expression cannot. In these pages, you will find poems that are personal, honest, and deeply felt. They are my attempt to give voice to the many emotions that arise in the wake of loss, and to offer a way forward towards healing and renewal.

It is my hope that this book will serve as a companion for those who are facing loss, and that it will offer a way to connect with the beauty and resilience that lies within us all.

ENDLESS CHILL

Amidst the depths of sorrow's sea,
The heart with grief is filled to be,
Its waves crash hard upon the shore,
And leave us stranded, sad and sore.

The world goes on, but we are still,
Enveloped in this endless chill,
A fog that shrouds our every thought,
And leaves us feeling lost and wrought.

The tears we cry, they fall like rain,
A never-ending source of pain,
They soak our souls and weigh us down,
As we stumble on this path, unbound.

We seek the light, but darkness reigns,
And we are trapped within its chains,
Our minds in turmoil, lost in grief,
A never-ending, tortured belief.
The words we speak, they fail to heal,

Our wounded hearts, they cannot feel,
The depth of pain, the endless ache,
That comes with every breath we take.

So we retreat into ourselves,
And guard our hearts, like precious wealth,
And though we may appear just fine,
Inside, we're broken, lost in time.

But slowly, oh so slowly, we,
Begin to heal, and start to see,
That though our pain will never fade,
We can move forward, unafraid.
And in the end, we find that grief,
Can teach us things we can't conceive,
That through the pain, we learn to grow,
And find a peace we didn't know.

So let the tears fall, let the pain,
Wash over us, like cleansing rain,
For though the road is long and tough,
We will find joy, when we've had enough.

BROKEN OPEN: FINDING BEAUTY IN THE ASHES OF GRIEF

In the depths of sorrow's night
Grief descends, a heavy weight
A storm of emotions, a tempest's might
Tears fall, a never-ending spate

The heart beats with a broken rhythm
A shattered soul, aching to be healed
In this labyrinth of pain and prison
The heart's secrets are forever sealed

The mind is a maze, a twisted path
Memories, regrets, and what-ifs collide
The present is a cruel aftermath
Of a past that can never be denied

The future looms with uncertainty
A shadow of what once was bright
Hope flickers with fragility
A flame that struggles to ignite

Yet in the midst of this desolation
A seed of beauty, a spark of light
A reminder of love's preservation
Of memories that never take flight

For grief is not a singular journey
But a path that we all must tread
With each step, a new discovery
Of the love that lives, even when we're dead

So let the tears fall, let the heart ache
For it is in this pain that we find grace
A connection that we cannot fake
A reminder of life's fleeting embrace

A TAPESTRY OF GRIEF AND HOPE

Amidst the chaos of sorrow's storm
Grief descends with its heavy form
A weight that crushes, a burden to bear
Tearing apart the fabric of what was once fair

The heart beats with a shattered rhythm
A broken vessel, aching to be healed
In this maze of pain and prison
The heart's secrets are forever sealed

The mind is a tangled web, a maze
Thoughts, regrets, and what-ifs collide
The present is but a cruel aftermath
Of a past that can never be denied

The future looms with uncertainty
A shadow of what once was bright
Hope flickers with fragility
A flame that struggles to ignite

Yet in the depths of this desolation
A seed of beauty, a spark of light
A reminder of love's preservation
Of memories that never take flight

For grief is not a solitary journey
But a path we all must walk alone
With each step, a new discovery
Of the love that never leaves its throne

So let the tears fall, let the heart break
For it is in this pain that we find grace
A connection that we cannot fake
A reminder of life's fleeting embrace

In the echoes of grief, we find our way
A labyrinth of loss, a path we must pay
Broken open, we find the light of day
A tapestry of life, woven in shades of gray

TIDAL WAVE OF GRIEF: NAVIGATING LOSS AND HEALING

In the depths of sorrow's sea,
A tidal wave of grief engulfs me,
A force that shakes my very soul,
And leaves me lost, adrift, and whole.

The weight of loss, a crushing blow,
That leaves me stunned, with nowhere to go,
The memories of what once was,
A bittersweet and painful cause.

I try to swim against the tide,
But grief's strong current cannot be denied,
A raging storm that leaves me reeling,
A wounded heart, forever feeling.

Each day a battle, fought with pain,
A struggle to find peace again,
To heal the wounds that won't subside,
And learn to live with what's inside.

But through the darkness, a glimmer of light,
A hope that shines so pure and bright,
A love that lives on, never to depart,
Forever etched upon my heart.

And so I'll keep on swimming, keep on trying,
For in the midst of grief, there's no denying,
That life goes on, though never the same,
And in that truth, I'll find my aim.

SHATTERED YET RISING

Amidst the depths of sorrow and despair,
Grief, an unwelcome visitor, did appear.
With heavy steps and somber glare,
It lingered, casting shadows everywhere.

In its wake, a torrent of tears,
And a storm of emotions, fears.
For in the face of loss and pain,
The heart can hardly bear the strain.

Days turned to weeks, weeks to months,
As grief held fast, unyielding in its hunt.
Memories of what once was,
Now a source of anguish and loss.

Questions unanswered, doubts remain,
As the mind tries to make sense of the pain.
Yet, in the midst of all the grief and strife,
A glimmer of hope, a flicker of life.

For though the heart may ache and break,
And though the soul may tremble and shake,

There is a light that shines within,
A flame of hope that burns, refusing to dim.

So let us grieve, and let us mourn,
And let us hold on to the love we've known.
For though the journey may be long,
The heart will find a way to carry on.

And in the end, when all is said and done,
The grief will fade, and hope will come.
For though we may be shattered and torn,
We will rise again, and be reborn.

HOPE'S FLICKERING FLAME

In times of turmoil, when all seems lost,
And darkness threatens to engulf us whole,
There is a flickering flame that we must hold,
The flame of hope that can light the way.

It is a flame that burns so bright,
Yet so elusive, like a butterfly in flight,
It dances and flutters, teasingly out of reach,
But we must not despair, we must not breach.

For hope is the force that keeps us going,
When all else fails, and we're left not knowing,
It lifts us up, and carries us through,
It gives us the strength to start anew.

Hope is the promise of a better tomorrow,
A brighter future free from sorrow,
It is the dream that we dare to chase,
The beacon that leads us to a better place.

So hold on tight to hope's flickering flame,
Let it guide you, let it light your way,

For in its warmth, we can find the strength,
To overcome the darkest of days.

Bursting with possibility and perplexity,
Hope's flickering flame leads us to our destiny.

WHEN HOPE BURSTS FORTH

Hope, oh hope, you fickle friend,
With bursts of joy, you do descend,
From skies of blue to depths of soul,
Your mysteries perplex and console.

Like a flame, you dance and flicker,
In times of darkness, you're the elixir,
That keeps us going, keeps us alive,
With the promise of a future we'll thrive.

But in the midst of our despair,
You can be elusive, you're not always there,
You tease and tantalize, then slip away,
Leaving us to wonder, and to pray.

Yet still we cling to you, oh hope,
For in your presence, we can cope,
With all the trials that life may bring,
And soar on wings of faith and sing.

So here's to hope, our faithful guide,
In whom we trust, and in whom we confide,
May you always light our way,
And bring us to a brighter day.

FLAMES OF HOPE: IGNITING THE PATH TO A BETTER FUTURE

Hope is the light that shines in the dark,
A beacon of strength that guides us through.
It's the courage to keep moving forward,
Even when the road ahead seems askew.

Hope is the flame that never goes out,
A spark that ignites a fire within.
It's the belief that there's more to life,
That there's a greater purpose we can win.

Hope is the voice that whispers to us,
A gentle reminder of our dreams.
It's the encouragement we need to hear,
When life is not as easy as it seems.

Hope is the power that lifts us up,
A force that keeps us going strong.
It's the faith that we will find our way,
Even when the path seems too long.

Hope is the promise that tomorrow,
Will be brighter than today.
It's the assurance that we can create,
A better world in every way.

So hold on tight to hope, my friends,
And let it guide you through the night.
For with hope in our hearts and souls,
We can achieve anything in sight.

HEALING: A JOURNEY OF LIGHT AND SHADOW

In the depths of darkness, a seed is sown
And from that seed, a light is born
A flame that flickers, fragile and alone
But grows in strength, as each day is borne

The road to healing is long and steep
A path of thorns, that cuts so deep
But with each step, a heart can leap
Towards a brighter future, we must keep

The scars we carry, may never fade
But in their place, new life is made
From brokenness, a beauty is displayed
A soul reborn, from the ashes laid

The journey of healing is a dance
A weaving of pain, and hope, and chance
A song of love, that we must enhance
And hold onto, with a steadfast stance

In the midst of chaos, we find our calm
A place of stillness, where we belong
A sanctuary, to heal and grow strong
To rise above, and right the wrongs

So let us embrace, the shadows and light
The highs and lows, that make us right
And through it all, we will take flight
Towards healing, and a life so bright.

CLUTCHES OF SORROW: A JOURNEY TO HOPE

Sorrow, oh sorrow, how you cling to my soul,
With a grip so fierce, you refuse to let go.
You drown me in tears, and suffocate my breath,
Till I'm left with nothing, but a body of death.

Your touch is so cold, and your whispers so dark,
Like a never-ending night, with no sign of a spark.
You seep into my bones, and poison my mind,
And leave me with nothing, but a pain undefined.

You are the shadow that follows me everywhere,
The constant reminder of the cross that I bear.
You strip me of joy, and rob me of peace,
And leave me with nothing, but a heart that's diseased.

You are the storm that rages inside of my chest,
The hurricane winds that never seem to rest.
You tear at my soul, and rip me apart,
And leave me with nothing, but a shattered heart.

Oh, sorrow, why do you haunt me so?
Why do you refuse to let me go?
I search for a way out, but you hold me in chains,
And leave me with nothing, but a life full of pains.

Yet, in the midst of the darkness, a glimmer of light,
A faint ray of hope, shining ever so bright.
For though you may hold me, and refuse to release,
There is one who can free me, and bring me to peace.

So, I'll cling to that hope, and I'll fight through the pain,
For though sorrow may come, it will not remain.
And in the end, I'll emerge from the night,
Stronger and wiser, with a heart full of light.

JOURNEY TO HEALING: A TRANSFORMATIONAL PROCESS

In the depths of pain, I sought a cure,
A way to heal, to feel pure,
But all I found were shattered dreams,
And endless nights of silent screams.

The wounds were deep, the scars so raw,
I couldn't move, couldn't stand tall,
But then I saw a glimmer of light,
And felt a warmth within ignite.

I realized then that healing's not a task,
It's a journey, a journey that we must ask,
For help and guidance, love and grace,
To find the strength to keep the pace.

With each step, the burdens lift,
And we begin to feel a shift,
From darkness into a brighter day,
Where hope and faith can guide the way.

The road is long, and fraught with pain,
But in the end, we will regain,
The power to live, to love, to be,
And find a new sense of clarity.

So if you're lost and feel alone,
Remember that you're not on your own,
For there are others who've been there too,
And together, we can see it through.

Healing is not a destination,
But a process of transformation,
And in the end, we'll find our way,
To a brighter, happier, healing day.

ECHOES OF LOSS: HONOURING MEMORIES AND FINDING STRENGTH

The weight of loss, a burden heavy
A wound that cuts, a hurt unsteady
A chasm deep, a void unfilled
A heart that aches, a soul that's chilled

The ache of absence, a pain so raw
A love once had, now forever gone
The tears that fall, like rain in spring
The memories, a bittersweet sting

The echoes of laughter, now silent and still
The promises broken, a bitter pill
The touch once felt, now a distant dream
The love once shared, now torn at the seams

The emptiness, a void so vast
The questions unanswered, a shadow cast
The longing for what once was true
The hope that someday, it may renew

The journey of grief, a winding road
The pain, a burden that we all must hold
But in the midst of sorrow and despair
There's a glimmer of hope, a light that's there

For though the loss may never fade
And the hurt may always remain
We can find the strength to carry on
And cherish the memories, forever strong

So let us honour those we've lost
And keep their memory close at heart
For in their absence, we can still find
The love and joy that they left behind.

UNYIELDING STRENGTH: THE FIRE WITHIN

Strength is not a shield to wield,
A thing that's hard and unyielding,
It's not a fortress that's unsealed,
But a force that comes from feeling.

It's the courage to face your fears,
To stand tall when the world is dark,
To wipe away your bitter tears,
And keep going when it's stark.

Strength is the fire that burns within,
The passion that drives you forward,
The belief that you can always win,
Even when you're feeling cornered.

It's the faith that you can rise again,
No matter how far you may fall,
And the hope that helps you sustain,
When everything else seems small.

Strength is not just muscle and might,
It's a mindset that can't be beaten,
It's a spirit that's ready to fight,
No matter what the world has eaten.

So take heart, my friend, and know,
That strength is not a thing you find,
It's something that you must grow,
From the depths of your heart and mind.

ADAPTATION: THE DANCE WITH FATE

Adaptation, the art of change,
A skill that we all must arrange.
In life, we face many twists and turns,
Some we can control, others we must learn.

Adaptation, a dance with fate,
The ability to pivot and innovate.
To bend but not break, to adjust our sail,
To weather the storm and never fail.

Adaptation, a journey to self,
A process of growth, a path to wealth.
To shed old skins and embrace the new,
To let go of fear and push on through.

Adaptation, a tale of survival,
A test of our strength and our will.
To rise from the ashes and soar high,
To reach for the stars and touch the sky.

Adaptation, a force to be reckoned with,
A power that lies within.
To harness its might and wield its strength,
To conquer our fears and go to great lengths.

Adaptation, a gift to behold,
A treasure more precious than gold.
To live a life that's full and free,
To be all we can be, and adapt with glee.

SHATTERED REFLECTIONS: A POETIC ODYSSEY OF LOSS AND RESILIENCE

In the depths of night, I ponder and weep,
For loss has come and my heart does keep,
Aching and longing for what used to be,
But now is gone, forever free.

Memories flood my mind like a raging sea,
Each one bursting with intensity,
Perplexing me with their vivid hue,
And making me wish for one last view.

The smell of your perfume still lingers in the air,
Your touch, your voice, I can almost hear,
But when I reach out, you're no longer there,
And my heart breaks, beyond repair.

I try to move on, to leave the pain behind,
But every step reminds me of what I can't find,
The emptiness consumes me, day and night,
Leaving me lost, without a light.

Oh loss, you cruel and bitter foe,
Why must you haunt me, and never let go?
But perhaps in your absence, I can grow,
And find a way to mend, and let love flow.

So I'll hold onto the memories, and cherish them dear,
And though you're gone, you'll always be near,
In my heart, in my soul, forever here,
As I move forward, through joy and tears.

RESILIENCE: A JOURNEY OF THE HUMAN SPIRIT

In life, we face trials and strife
Obstacles that seem to cut like a knife
But deep within, there lies a fire
A flame that burns with fierce desire

Resilience is the force within
That keeps us going, despite the din
It's the ability to stand up tall
After every stumble and fall

It's the courage to face our fears
And wipe away the flowing tears
It's the strength to carry on
When all our hopes seem gone

Resilience is not a gift bestowed
But a trait that can be honed and grown
It's the product of our struggles and pain
That helps us rise up again and again

Life's challenges may seem unending
But with resilience, we keep transcending
Our limits and fears, and rise above
To embrace the beauty of life and love

So let us cherish this spirit within
And use it to overcome every sin
Let us rise up, like a phoenix from the ash
And live our lives with hope and dash

For resilience is the human spirit
That can weather every storm and merit
And take us to places we never dreamed
Where the impossible becomes the redeemed.

ECHOES OF SORROW: A JOURNEY THROUGH GRIEF

Amidst the depths of sorrow's sea,
Where waves of grief do crash and heave,
The heart is torn, the soul does grieve,
And words escape, unable to be.

In pain and anguish, lost in thought,
The mind cannot comprehend the loss,
The heart aches with a heavy cost,
And memories flood, the soul distraught.

The tears that fall, like rain in spring,
Wash away the pain and sting,
But never can they truly bring,
Relief from sorrow's everlasting ring.

And so we mourn, in silence and woe,
Our loved ones lost, forever ago,
The pain remains, a constant flow,
In grief's embrace, we ebb and grow.

Yet amidst the darkness, a light does shine,
A glimmer of hope, a sacred sign,
That in time, the heart will align,
With love and peace, a new design.

So let us mourn, but also hope,
For in grief's grasp, we learn to cope,
And through the pain, we find a way to elope,
From sorrow's grip, to a brighter slope.

RESILIENCE: A POEM OF TRIUMPH

Through the storms of life, we must endure
The winds of change, the trials obscure
For though we may falter, we shall not fall
For we are made of stronger stuff, after all

Our hearts may break, our souls may cry
But we must keep on, we must defy
The darkness that threatens to consume
For we are not defeated, we shall resume

Our path may be twisted, our journey long
But we must keep on, we must stay strong
For though the road may be steep and rough
We shall not give up, we shall not give up

For we are the warriors of our own fate
We are the masters of our own faith
And though the world may try to break us
We shall not yield, we shall not fuss

For we are the embodiment of resilience
The very essence of strength and persistence
And through the battles we may face
We shall emerge victorious, with grace

So let us stand tall, let us stand proud
Let us face our challenges, unbowed
For we are the champions of our own lives
And with resilience, we shall thrive.

DANCE OF RESILIENCE: THE SYMPHONY OF STRENGTH

Resilience is a dance
Of chaos and order,
A symphony of strength
In moments of disorder.

It's the will to rise up
When life knocks you down,
To stand in the face of pain
And refuse to drown.

It's the voice that whispers,
"You can make it through,"
When the road ahead
Seems long and daunting to pursue.

It's the flame that flickers,
But never fully dies,
A beacon of hope
That keeps the spirit alive.

Resilience is not easy,
But it's worth the fight,
For it holds the power
To turn darkness into light.

So when life throws you curves,
And you feel like giving in,
Remember that resilience
Is the ultimate win.

For it's in the toughest moments,
That we find our greatest strength,
And in the face of adversity,
We learn to go to great length.

So take a deep breath,
And hold your head up high,
For with resilience as your guide,
You can conquer any sky.

UNBREAKABLE: THE RESILIENT HEART

Resilience, the steel within,
Forged by flames of pain and sin.
A force that rises from the ashes,
And overcomes life's brutal lashes.

The winds may howl, the skies may weep,
But the resilient heart does not sleep.
It beats with strength and unwavering might,
Guided by the will to survive the night.

The storms may rage, the earth may quake,
But the resilient spirit does not break.
It stands tall, unyielding and true,
Fueled by a fierce determination to push through.

Resilience, the warrior's shield,
That never fades, never yields.
A power that transforms defeat into victory,
And turns adversity into a tale of glory.

So let us embrace the trials we face,
And meet them with resilience and grace.
For in the face of life's greatest tests,
It is the resilient heart that stands the best.

WHISPERS OF ABSENCE

In the quiet of the night,
I hear the whispers of your name.
The memories flood my mind,
And the pain, it feels the same.

I reach out to touch your face,
But my fingers grasp at air.
Your absence is a void,
A wound that won't repair.

I try to make sense of it all,
The reasons why you had to go.
But the answers, they elude me,
A puzzle I can't seem to know.

The world spins on without you,
And I'm left here to mourn.
The ache inside me deepens,
As I face another dawn.

The tears they flow like rivers,
And my heart, it feels so raw.

The weight of your absence,
A burden that I can't ignore.

But through the pain and sorrow,
I hold on to the memories we shared.
And though you may be gone,
Your love, it still is here.

In the quiet of the night,
I whisper to the sky above.
For even though you're gone,
Your presence, it still fills my love.

LOVE ENDURES BEYOND LOSS

Love endures beyond the pain of loss,
A flame that burns despite the frost,
A memory that lingers on and on,
Long after the loved one is gone.

The heart may ache, the tears may fall,
But love remains through it all,
A bond that time can never break,
A light that darkness cannot take.

Though life may seem so dark and drear,
Love shines through, so bright and clear,
A beacon in the stormy night,
Guiding us to a new daylight.

Love is a mystery, complex and deep,
A riddle that we cannot keep,
A burst of joy, a sea of tears,
A feeling that defies our fears.

And though we may not understand,
The power of love across the land,
We know that it endures all things,
And in our hearts forever sings.

So let us cherish what we've had,
And hold love close, even when we're sad,
For in its presence we find strength,
To carry on through any length.

Love endures beyond the pain of loss,
And in its glow we find our boss,
Guiding us through every trial,
To find our way through the miles.

LOVE STILL PRESENT DESPITE LOSS

In the darkness of my grief,
I thought my heart would never heal,
But even as I wept and mourned,
Love remained, a steadfast seal.

I thought I'd lost you forever,
That your absence would be a void,
But in the quiet of my heart,
Your love remained, unalloyed.

I searched for you in memories,
In the things we used to share,
But it wasn't until I looked within,
That I found you waiting there.

Your love is like a secret garden,
Hidden in the depths of me,
And though you're gone, it still blooms,
A fragrant, vibrant, living tree.

In every whispered thought of you,
In every gentle breeze that blows,
I feel your presence all around,
And love still blooms, despite the woes.

So though you may have left this world,
And though my heart may ache and cry,
Love remains, a constant light,
Guiding me, until we reunite.

ETERNAL FLAME: LOVE THAT ENDURES BEYOND LOSS

In the depths of my heart, a flame still burns,
Though you are gone, my love, my soul still yearns,
For the warmth of your touch, the sound of your voice,
The way you made my heart rejoice.

The memories we shared, the love we knew,
Are etched forever in my heart, like morning dew,
Glistening in the sun, reflecting all the love we had,
And reminding me of the happiness that once made me glad.

The pain of losing you is sharp, like a knife,
But my love for you endures, despite the strife,
It lives on in my heart, a flame that cannot die,
For even in death, our love will never say goodbye.

The world may move on, and time may heal the wound,
But my love for you will never be consumed,
By the flames of grief, or the darkness of night,
For our love was pure, and its light will always shine bright.

So though you may be gone, and I may be alone,
My love for you remains, like a precious stone,
A testament to the power of love, to endure and survive,
And a symbol of the truth that true love never dies.

GHOSTS OF LOVE

In the deep of night when all is still,
When memories haunt and thoughts distill,
When tears fall freely, unchecked and raw,
Love remains, despite loss and flaw.

It lingers on in the scent of sheets,
In the echoes of laughter, bittersweet,
In the warmth of a touch long gone,
In the whispered words of a love song.

It survives the trials of time and space,
The distance between us, the empty place,
The silence that fills the once busy room,
The absence that lingers, a constant gloom.

Love endures the pain of goodbye,
The ache of a heart that cannot deny,
The longing for a love that was true,
The hope that one day, it will renew.

It's the burst of light in a darkened sky,
The rainbow that arches, the butterfly,

The unexpected smile from a stranger,
The reminder that love is not a danger.

Love is the perplexity of life,
The mystery that cuts like a knife,
The answer to questions we cannot ask,
The light that shines through a broken mask.

So let love remain, despite the loss,
Let it fill the heart, let it be the boss,
Let it guide us through the unknown,
Let it be the place we call home.

LOVE ENDURES

Amidst the ruins of my broken heart,
Love's ember still flickers, though torn apart.
The ache of loss is a bitter pill,
Yet memories of love sustain me still.

The echoes of your laughter and your smile,
Haunt me, comfort me, all the while.
A ghostly presence that I cannot shake,
Reminding me of the love we used to make.

In sleepless nights, I hear your voice,
As if you're here, but it's just a choice.
To cling to love that's now a memory,
A twisted fate, a cruel destiny.

But still I hold on to the love we shared,
And in my heart, you're always there.
Though time may pass and wounds may heal,
Love endures, a love that's real.

So though you're gone, I'll never forget,
The love we had, the love that met.
And though I'm broken, I'll rise again,
For love endures, forever and amen.

ETERNAL BOND

In the depths of my heart, a void so vast,
A wound so deep, it's hard to surpass,
My mother, my guide, my beacon of light,
Taken away, leaving me in endless night.

Her love, her warmth, her gentle touch,
Memories flood my mind, I miss her so much,
The scent of her perfume, her smile so bright,
Reminds me of her, day and night.

Her absence, a weight I can't bear,
My heart aches, as if it's beyond repair,
The world feels bleak, devoid of all cheer,
For nothing can replace a mother so dear.

Her wisdom, her counsel, her comforting ways,
Are etched in my soul, for all of my days,
Though she's gone, her spirit remains,
In every beat of my heart, in all of my veins.

I'll carry on, but I'll always miss,
The one who gave me life, my greatest bliss,
A mother's love, so pure and true,
I'll forever cherish, and hold onto.

So here I am, with a heart so raw,
Paying homage to the one I adore,
My mother, my rock, my everything,
Who taught me to love, to laugh, to sing.

Though she's gone, she'll never truly leave,
For her legacy lives on, in all that I believe,
And in this loss, I find my strength,
For my mother's love, will go to any length.

FOREVER IN MY HEART

As I look upon the empty chair
Where once my father sat with care,
I feel a weight upon my soul,
A loss that leaves me less whole.

The memories flood my mind,
Of times we laughed and were so kind,
But now he's gone, and I'm left behind,
Alone in grief, with naught to find.

The words I seek evade me so,
My heart is heavy, my thoughts slow,
But in this sorrow, I must grow,
To find a way to let it go.

The tears I shed are bittersweet,
A reminder of what we cannot meet,
Yet in my heart, his love still beats,
Guiding me through the ups and the heats.

Oh, father, how I miss you so,
But in my heart, you'll always glow,

A shining star that guides me through,
A love that's forever true.

Though your physical form is gone,
Your spirit lives and carries on,
And in your absence, I'll be strong,
For you, my father, forever long.

So here's to you, my dearest dad,
Your love and light will never fade,
And though I miss you, I'm so glad,
For the time we shared, the memories made.

LAST EMBRACE: A POEM OF FAREWELL AND HOPE

In the last embrace before loss,
we clasp each other tight,
Our love a fierce and burning flame,
That soon will flicker out of sight.

We hold on tight with all our might,
As time begins to slip away,
Our tears they flow, our hearts they break,
As we know we'll soon be led astray.

Our memories flood back, like waves,
Of all the moments we have shared,
And yet we know that all too soon,
Those moments will no longer be there.

The burst of pain, so sharp and deep,
It takes our breath away,
We wonder how we'll bear the loss,
As we prepare to face the day.

Perplexity fills our hearts and minds,
As we struggle to understand,
How life can be so fleeting,
And slip away just like sand.

But in this last embrace before loss,
We find a glimmer of hope,
For love endures beyond the grave,
And helps us to learn and to cope.

So though we grieve and weep and mourn,
For what we've lost and what we'll miss,
We hold on to the love we shared,
And cherish each and every kiss.

LOVE'S LEGACY: FINDING PEACE AFTER LOSS

Amidst the silence of the night,
With tears that fall like rain,
I bid farewell to my beloved,
Whose soul has been set free again.

The ache inside me is unbearable,
My heart shattered into a million pieces,
Yet I find solace in knowing,
That my loved one is now at peace.

The memories of our time together,
Haunt me like a bittersweet dream,
And I am torn between sorrow and gratitude,
For having loved and been loved, it seems.

But in the midst of this pain,
I find a glimmer of hope,
For in death, there is peace,
And a chance for a new beginning to cope.

The void left by my loved one,
Cannot be filled by anyone else,
But in their passing, they have left me,
With a legacy of love that will never fade away.

So I bid farewell to my beloved,
With a heavy heart, yet a sense of relief,
For they are now at peace at last,
And their love will always be my guiding belief.

And though my grief may linger,
I know that peace will come,
For in the end, love conquers all,
And in that, I find comfort in the sum.

ETERNAL LIGHT: A TRIBUTE TO MY GRANDMOTHER

As I sit and reminisce on days gone by,
My heart aches, for my dear grandmother has passed by.
Her smile, her warmth, her gentle embrace,
All now just memories, that time cannot replace.

She was the rock, the foundation of our family,
Guiding us with love and unwavering loyalty.
Her words were wisdom, her actions pure,
Her kindness and grace, forever will endure.

But now she's gone, and my heart is heavy,
The pain I feel, unbearable and unsteady.
The world seems dimmer, less vibrant than before,
For she was the light that shone evermore.

I cannot fathom life without her by my side,
No longer able to seek her wisdom, or confide.
The thought of never seeing her smile again,
Causes my heart to ache, my soul to bend.

Yet through the pain, I feel her love still,
A love that time and death cannot kill.
Her spirit lives on, in every memory and thought,
And though she's gone, her love cannot be bought.

So I'll hold onto her memory, with all my might,
And cherish the moments we shared, day and night.
For though she's gone, she'll never truly leave,
Her love and light, forever will weave.

THE ETERNAL FLAME OF LOVE

In the stillness of night,
I feel your presence near,
Though you're gone from sight,
Your love I hold dear.

Your soul has departed,
But our love still remains,
In my heart it's imparted,
A never-ending flame.

The foundation we built,
Stands strong even in death,
Our love will not wilt,
As long as I have breath.

The memories we shared,
Are like stars in the sky,
Bright and sparkling,
Never to die.

The pain of your loss,
I cannot deny,
But in my heart you toss,
A love that will never die.

So even though you're gone,
Our love will endure,
In my heart it lives on,
Everlasting and pure.

For the foundation of love,
Is not bound by time,
It transcends all,
Even after we've left behind.

And so I'll hold onto,
The love we once shared,
For even in death,
It's a love that's still there.

ETERNAL FOUNDATIONS: LOVE BEYOND DEATH

In the depths of sorrow and grief,
When all seems lost beyond belief,
A foundation of love remains,
A steadfast bond that forever sustains.

Death may take our mortal shell,
But love endures and will always dwell,
In memories that we hold dear,
And in the hearts of those we're near.

Beneath the soil and stone,
Love's foundation is firmly sewn,
Rooted deep in the earth below,
Yet soaring high like a heavenly glow.

Through the veil that separates,
Love transcends and never abates,
Like a spark that ignites the night,
Love shines on with eternal light.

And though our bodies may decay,
Love's foundation will never sway,
For in death we are but transformed,
Our spirits free, our love reformed.

So let us celebrate the love we share,
And cherish it with utmost care,
For in life and even in death,
Love's foundation never fades, never rests.

RISING STRONG: POETRY OF PERSEVERANCE AND COURAGE

Resilience is a force that can't be tamed
A strength that emerges from hardship and pain
It's a light that shines even in the darkest of nights
And a spirit that never gives up without a fight

It's a flower that blooms in the harshest terrain
And a seed that sprouts after the fiercest of rains
It's a phoenix that rises from the ashes of defeat
And a heartbeat that never admits defeat

Resilience is a flame that burns bright and true
A beacon that guides us when we don't know what to do
It's a rope that pulls us out of the deepest of holes
And a whisper that reminds us we're not alone

It's a shield that protects us from the storms of life
And a ladder that helps us climb the highest of heights
It's a song that fills us with hope and inspiration
And a love that fuels us with determination

Resilience is a symphony of courage and grace
A symphony that never fades or loses its place
It's a dance that weaves through the ups and the downs
And a story that reminds us we're capable of profound

So let us embrace our resilience with open hearts
And let us never forget its power to transform
For it is the key to overcoming every obstacle
And the secret to living a life that is unstoppable.

LETTING GO

Letting go is a mighty feat,
A journey that we all must meet.
It's shedding skin, it's breaking free,
It's learning how to just let be.

It's saying goodbye to what was once held dear,
And embracing the unknown without fear.
It's trusting that the universe will guide our way,
Even when the path seems unclear each day.

Letting go is a constant practice,
A dance between surrender and defiance.
It's learning to release our grip,
And finding peace in the letting slip.

It's understanding that what we release,
Is not always gone, but simply at ease.
It's learning to appreciate the memories,
And finding solace in the bittersweet reveries.

Letting go is a powerful act,
A journey that can leave us cracked.

But it's in the cracks that light can seep,
And in the darkness that we learn to see.

So let us embrace the letting go,
And trust that our hearts will continue to grow.
For in the release, we find our strength,
And in the freedom, we find our breadth.

ECHOES OF DEPARTURE

As I walk the lonely path of grief,
I see the footprints left behind,
By those who walked this way before,
Their stories lost, but footprints remain.

The sand beneath my feet is soft,
But the weight of loss is heavy,
Each step I take feels like a burden,
But I must keep moving forward.

The footprints I see are varied,
Some deep and well-defined,
Others barely there, almost faded,
But all telling stories of loss and pain.

There are footprints of those who left,
Without a chance to say goodbye,
Footprints of those who suffered,
And left this world with tears in their eyes.

I follow the footprints with caution,
Afraid of what I might find,

But still, I keep walking, hoping,
That someday, peace I will find.

The footprints lead me to a place,
Where I can finally let go,
Of the pain that's been holding me back,
And the burden that's been weighing me down.

As I stand there, looking back,
At the footprints I've left behind,
I realize that every step I took,
Was a step towards healing and light.

And though the journey was hard,
And the road was full of pain,
I'm grateful for the footprints left behind,
And the hope they bring again.

ABSENCE OF A GUIDING LIGHT

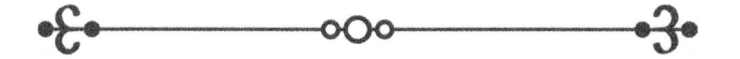

In the silence of the night, I hear your voice,
Echoing through the emptiness that was once filled with your presence.
My heart aches with the loss of you, my father,
And my mind is consumed with the memories of our time together.

I see you in my dreams, but wake up to an empty reality,
A reality where I must learn to navigate without your guidance.
Your absence leaves me lost and alone,
But your love remains with me, a constant reminder of the bond we shared.

The tears that I shed are a testament to the pain I feel,
A pain that words can't express, a pain that only the heart can understand.
But even in my sorrow, I find comfort in the thought of you,
And the knowledge that you are always with me, watching over me from above.

I remember the lessons you taught me, the values you instilled in me,

And I hold onto them tightly, as if they were physical treasures.
For though you may be gone, your legacy lives on in me,
And in the lives of those you touched during your time on
this earth.

So I say goodbye to you, my father, with a heavy heart,
But with the knowledge that our love will never truly die.
For even in death, you remain a part of me,
And I will honor your memory by living a life that would make
you proud.

A MOTHER'S LIGHT

She was the light that shone so bright,
A beacon of hope in the darkest night.
She was the one who held us close,
Her love and warmth like a fragrant rose.

But now she's gone, and we're alone,
Lost in a world that's so unknown.
Her absence is like a gaping hole,
A wound that cuts deep into the soul.

The memories we have, they linger on,
A bittersweet reminder of what's gone.
We try to hold on to every last trace,
Of the love she gave us in every embrace.

But time goes by, and life moves on,
And we realize that she's truly gone.
The pain we feel, it never ends,
A wound that never quite mends.

Yet still we find a way to carry on,
To live our lives, and to be strong.

For she lives on in every memory,
And in the love that we still carry.

So though we miss her every day,
We know she wouldn't want us to stay,
Lost in grief, consumed by loss,
She'd want us to live, and to love at any cost.

For she was the light that shone so bright,
And though she's gone, she's still our guide.
Her love and warmth will always be,
The light that helps us to see.

So we'll carry on, and we'll hold tight,
To the memories of our mother's light.
For though she's gone, she's never far,
And her love will always be our guiding star.

THE EVER-EVOLVING DANCE OF LIFE

Adaptation, a dance with change,
An art form of fluidity, not estrange.
With each step, a new path to forge,
A journey of growth, a chance to gorge.

The unknown is daunting, yet we persist,
With resilience and courage, we do exist.
We bend and sway with the winds of time,
An ever-evolving, mesmerizing mime.

Adaptation, a process of transformation,
A metamorphosis, a grand revelation.
We shed our old selves, to be reborn anew,
A cycle of growth, a transformational view.

The journey is bumpy, with twists and turns,
A maze of uncertainty, where the heart yearns.
Yet, we forge ahead, with a spirit unbroken,
A fearless pursuit, of dreams unspoken.

Adaptation, a test of our inner strength,
A chance to find purpose, to go to great lengths.
To conquer the obstacles, and reach new heights,
A symphony of life, with all its delights.

So let us embrace the unknown with grace,
And dance to the rhythm of change's pace.
For adaptation is a beautiful song,
A never-ending, yet wondrous lifelong.

THE LASTING PRESENCE OF GRANDFATHER

Amidst the quiet whispers of time,
A loss so great, a mountain to climb.
My grandfather, my guide, my friend,
His presence now, a memory to fend.

The world now seems so cold and bare,
His gentle voice, no longer there.
The laughter and the stories he shared,
With every moment, now ensnared.

The house, once filled with his embrace,
Now echoes with an empty space.
The warmth he brought, now long gone,
Leaves me feeling so very alone.

But though he's gone, his spirit lives,
In every moment that time gives.
His wisdom and his love remain,
A legacy that will forever sustain.

And though the pain may never fade,
The memories of him will never evade.
For in my heart, he'll always be,
A cherished part of my family tree.

Oh, grandfather, how I miss you so,
But in my heart, your love will always glow.
For though you've left this mortal plane,
Your spirit and your light will forever reign.

A MOTHER'S REFLECTIONS ON LOSS

In the stillness of the night,
Her tears fall like gentle rain.
The world is dark, and all is quiet,
But her heart is filled with pain.

She mourns the loss of her child,
Whose life was cut too short.
The memories of their love and laughter
Are all that she can now resort.

She wanders through the empty rooms,
And touches each treasured thing.
The clothes, the toys, the photographs
All bring back the joy they bring.

She wonders how to carry on
Without the one she loves.
Her heart is heavy, and her soul is tired,
And her thoughts are dark as dusk.

But through her grief, she finds a way
To honor her child's memory.
She speaks of them with pride and love,
And in her heart, they'll always be.

For though they're gone, they're still with her
In every beat of her heart.
And though she mourns, she knows their love
Will never truly depart.

So let her weep, and let her mourn,
For loss is a heavy weight.
But let her also remember love,
For that will always remain.

THE WEIGHT OF BROTHER'S LOSS

In the stillness of the night,
My heart aches with a bitter plight,
As I mourn the loss of my dear brother,
Whose absence feels like a stab to my mother.

The memories we shared, so vivid and bright,
Now seem like a distant and fading light,
As I struggle to come to terms,
With the finality of his earthly terms.

His laughter, his smile, his infectious charm,
Are now forever lost, causing great harm,
To my soul, my spirit, my very being,
Leaving me feeling alone and unseeing.

Oh, how I long for one more day,
To hear his voice and see his face,
To feel his embrace and hold him tight,
To tell him that everything will be alright.

I try to hold on to the moment,
To savor every last sensation,
But the ache within my heart is growing,
As I feel the weight of separation.

And then you pull away from me,
A tear upon your cheek,
And I know that this is truly it,
The end of what we seek.

So I stand there, alone and broken,
As you walk away from me,
And in my heart, I know that this,
Was the last embrace we'll ever be.

CONQUERING THE SHADOW

Cancer, the thief of life,
Stealing away our days,
A shadow lurking in the dark,
A monster we can't escape.

It strikes with sudden fury,
Tearing families apart,
Leaving pain and sorrow,
Etched forever on our hearts.

We try to fight it with all our might,
Chemo, radiation, surgery,
But sometimes it's just not enough,
And we're left with nothing but misery.

Yet even in the darkest moments,
There's a glimmer of hope,
A light that shines within us all,
A strength we never knew we could hold.

We come together in solidarity,
To lift each other up,

To stand strong in the face of adversity,
And never, ever give up.

So let us hold onto that hope,
And keep fighting every day,
Until we conquer this disease,
And cancer fades away.

RESILIENCE AMIDST TRAGEDY

Tragedy, oh tragedy, why must you always be
A weight that we carry, a burden we can't flee
Your arrival is sudden, your departure unsure
Leaving us in a state of chaos, shaken to the core

Like a storm that rages, you tear apart our lives
Leaving us with nothing, but shattered dreams and strife
Our hearts ache with sorrow, our souls consumed with pain
As we struggle to make sense of what we can't explain

Tragedy, oh tragedy, you come in many forms
A lover's betrayal, a child's illness, a soldier's uniform
You strike without warning, you leave us in despair
Our lives forever altered, our hopes left to wither and tear

But even in the darkest moments, when all seems lost
We find a glimmer of hope, a light that we can't exhaust
For within the tragedy, there is a strength that we find
A resilience that carries us forward, a spirit that won't resign

Tragedy, oh tragedy, you test us in many ways
But we will not be broken, we will rise above the fray

For in the face of adversity, we find our truest selves
And though you may have struck us down, we will not be quelled.

THE WEIGHT OF WAR

In the midst of war, we stand,
Our hearts heavy, our souls burdened,
We mourn the loss of those we loved,
Their absence a constant reminder of the cost of battle.

We cry out to the heavens, asking why,
Why must so many suffer and die,
Why must families be torn apart,
Why must we carry the weight of loss in our hearts?

The pain is raw, the wound is deep,
The memories of those we've lost forever we'll keep,
Their laughter, their smiles, their gentle touch,
All now memories, the past we clutch.

The world is different now, forever changed,
The scars of war, in our minds ingrained,
We mourn the loss of a world once bright,
Now shrouded in darkness, in endless night.

We pray for peace, for an end to the fight,
For a world where love can once again take flight,

For a future where our children can be free,
And the only loss we know is the loss of memory.

But until then, we'll remember those we've lost,
Their names forever etched in stone at great cost,
Their sacrifice a reminder of the price we pay,
For the freedom we cherish, day by day.

So let us mourn, let us grieve,
For the loss of those we loved and believed,
Let us honor their memory, let us never forget,
That in the face of war, we must stand together, lest we too, are met with regret.

TENDER TEARS: A POEM OF LOVE AND LOSS FOR MOURNING PARENTS

In the stillness of the night,
The heart aches with a terrible might,
For parents mourned, too soon gone,
Leaving behind a world undone.

Their absence felt in every breath,
The pain of loss, a lingering death,
Memories flood in, both sweet and sad,
Of moments shared, both good and bad.

The weight of grief, a heavy load,
A path unknown, an untrodden road,
Their love and care, a treasure rare,
Their presence felt everywhere.

The tears that fall, a river wide,
A flood of sorrow, that cannot hide,
Their absence felt in every beat,
A pain that never will retreat.

Their legacy lives on, in every way,
Their love and warmth, forever to stay,
Though they are gone, their spirit remains,
Guiding us through life's many pains.

Mourning parents, a bittersweet pain,
A loss that forever will remain,
But in their memory, we find hope,
And with their love, we learn to cope.

ECHOES OF A MOURNING SOULMATE

In the depths of my sorrow, I mourn,
For my soulmate, forever gone.
My heart aches with each passing day,
As I struggle to find my way.

The memories we shared flood my mind,
Leaving me lost and undefined.
The laughter, the love, the tears we shed,
Are now nothing but echoes in my head.

My soul cries out, aching for his touch,
But he's nowhere to be found, not even a clutch.
The emptiness consumes me whole,
As I wander, searching for my soul.

The stars in the sky, they twinkle and shine,
But they can't bring him back, they can't be mine.
The burst of light, the burst of hope,
Now nothing but an elusive trope.

The world around me keeps moving on,
But I'm stuck in this moment, frozen and alone.
The perplexity of life without him,
Has left me broken, shattered, and grim.

So I mourn my soulmate, forevermore,
And hold onto memories, like never before.
For he will always be a part of me,
And our love will live on, for eternity

FOREVER IN MY HEART: A POEM ON THE UNFORGETTABLE LOVE OF A MOTHER

In the depth of night, I lie awake,
Tears streaming down my face,
As memories of you flood my mind,
And the pain of your loss I cannot erase.

You were the light of my life,
The one who always understood,
Your gentle touch and kind heart,
Were the only things that ever could.

Now that you're gone, I feel so lost,
In a world that seems so dark and cold,
And I wonder how I'll ever find my way,
Without you to guide me as I grow old.

I miss the sound of your voice,
The warmth of your embrace,

The way you made everything alright,
With just a smile upon your face.

But though you're no longer with me,
I feel your presence all around,
In the whisper of the wind,
In the beauty of the sunset's crown.

For though you're gone, you're never far,
Your love will always be my guide,
And in my heart, you'll live forever,
As the most precious part of me inside.

So though I may shed tears of sorrow,
And feel the pain of your loss each day,
I know that you're watching over me,
And that your love will never fade away.

SUDDEN PASSING

In the blink of an eye, a life can end,
A soul released, free to transcend,
From this world of sorrows and pain,
To a place where peace and love reign.

No warning given, no chance to prepare,
A sudden death, life's ultimate dare,
Leaves loved ones shocked, confused, and numb,
Their hearts shattered, their futures undone.

Questions arise, unanswerable, perplexing,
Why did this happen? What was the reckoning?
Could we have done something, anything at all,
To prevent this tragedy, this untimely fall?

The burst of emotions, a turbulent ride,
From disbelief to anger, from sorrow to pride,
Memories flood in, of times gone by,
Of laughter, of love, of tears that we cried.

But in the midst of the chaos, a glimmer of light,
A reminder that death is a natural rite,

That life is fleeting, and every moment counts,
That we should cherish our loved ones, without any doubts.

So let us grieve, let us mourn,
Let us celebrate a life that was born,
Let us remember the joy, the love, the laughter,
And let us carry on, for that is what truly matters.

MEMORIES THAT ENDURE

In the depths of sorrow and the grip of pain,
Memories flood my mind like an endless rain,
The ones I loved and lost, they haunt me still,
Their voices echo in my heart, with an ache that could kill.

The scent of their presence, the touch of their hand,
The warmth of their embrace, now lost to the sand,
Their faces etched in my mind, like a vivid dream,
But now only memories, in my heart they gleam.

The pain of loss, it cuts so deep,
A wound that never truly heals or sleeps,
But through the tears and the heartache,
Their memory lives on, never to forsake.

The laughter we shared, the moments we cherished,
Their spirit lives on, forever nourished,
By the love that we gave and the love that we received,
Their memory alive, never to be deceived.

So though they may be gone, they remain in our hearts,
Their legacy lives on, never to depart,

For love is the bond that connects us still,
Their memory endures, forever and until.

And though the pain of loss may never go away,
Their memory brings comfort, day by day,
For in the moments we shared, they will always be,
A part of us forever, for eternity.

FADING LIGHT: A POEM ON THE WORSENING HEALTH OF A LOVED ONE

The sun still rises, the world still turns,
But my heart is heavy, my spirit yearns.
For the health of my loved one, so dear,
Whose body betrays them, year after year.

They were once strong, full of life and vigor,
But now they struggle, their breath growing thinner.
Their once bright eyes are now dull and hazy,
Their once steady hands now shake and quiver.

I watch them suffer, day after day,
As their body slowly withers away.
I try to offer comfort and care,
But my heart is heavy with despair.

The doctors offer treatments and pills,
But they do little to ease their ills.
The prognosis is grim, the outlook bleak,
And each day feels like a mountain to peak.

I pray for a miracle, a cure, a way,
To turn back time, to make them okay.
But the truth is harsh, and the reality clear,
That their worsening health is something to fear.

I hold their hand, and I whisper soft,
That they are loved, and never forgot.
That even as their body fails,
Their spirit soars, and their heart prevails.

So I'll cherish each moment, each fleeting breath,
And hold onto hope, even in the face of death.
For the love we share is a bond unbreakable,
And it will carry us through, even when things seem impossible.

HAUNTING SHADOWS: A JOURNEY THROUGH TRAUMA

Trauma, oh trauma, you elusive beast
You haunt my every waking thought
A burden I cannot release

You creep up on me in the dead of night
And haunt my dreams with all your might
Your tendrils reach into my soul
And leave me feeling far from whole

The memories you bring are sharp and raw
And leave me feeling lost and small
My mind is filled with fear and pain
And I wonder if I'll ever be whole again

You twist and turn inside my brain
And I can't escape your endless reign
My thoughts are scattered, wild and free
And I wonder who I'll ever be

But through it all, I hold on tight
To the hope that someday I'll see the light
That I'll find my way out of the dark
And find some peace within my heart

So trauma, oh trauma, I'll face you head on
I'll keep moving forward until you're gone
And though you've left me bruised and scarred
I'll rise above and shine like a star.

ECHOES OF SOLITUDE: GRIEVING THE LOSS OF LOVE

Amidst the empty space and vacant air,
I stand alone, a lonely soul laid bare.
My heart still aches from loss and pain,
The memories of a love that will never reign.

The silence echoes loudly in my mind,
As I search for solace that I can't find.
My tears have dried, my eyes have wept,
My spirit crushed, my dreams have crept.

I scream out loud, but no one hears,
My cries lost in the emptiness of my fears.
The world moves on, but I stand still,
My heart shattered, my soul unfulfilled.

I long for warmth, for a loving touch,
But all I feel is an endless clutch,
Of loneliness and sorrow that won't subside,
As I grieve the loss of the one who died.

The nights are long, the days are bleak,
My shattered heart feels so weak,
The pain so deep, the hurt so raw,
My life forever changed by this great flaw.

So I stand alone, in this empty place,
Searching for meaning and a way to face,
The loneliness that haunts me day and night,
After losing my love, my heart's only light.

But though I feel the weight of this great loss,
I know that life goes on, no matter the cost.
And so I keep on moving, one step at a time,
Trusting that someday, my heart will once again shine.

LOVE BEYOND THE VEIL

In death we part, but love endures
Beyond the veil that death secures
For love is not bound by earthly ties
It soars on wings that reach the skies

The flame of love may dim and fade
But death cannot its power invade
For love transcends this mortal plane
And in our hearts forever reigns

In life we laugh, in life we cry
But love remains until we die
And even then it lingers on
A flame that never can be gone

So fear not death, my love, my friend
For though our time on earth must end
Our love will last through all of time
And in the next life, we'll be fine

For love is not a fleeting thing
But an eternal, ever-spring

That bursts forth in a dazzling light
And fills our hearts with pure delight

So let us love with all our might
Until the day turns into night
And then beyond, in death's embrace
Our love will shine in timeless grace.

MOURNING'S EMBRACE

Oh, sorrow's grasp, so fierce and cold,
Envelops me in mourning's hold.
My heart, once full of light and mirth,
Now shattered by this pain and dearth.
How can I bear this weight so heavy,
When every breath feels thick and levee?
My soul is wracked with bitter grief,
And I'm lost in a world of disbelief.

The memories flood my troubled mind,
Of happier days left far behind.
The laughter, love, and joy we shared,
All vanished now, beyond repair.
I wander through this endless night,
Seeking solace, seeking light.
But all I find is emptiness,
And the echoes of my own distress.

How can I go on without you here,
When every day is filled with fear?
The thought of living without your touch,
Is almost more than I can bear.

And yet, within this mourning's hold,
I feel a spark of hope unfold.
A glimmer of the love we knew,
That still remains, forever true.

Though you are gone, I hold you near,
And in my heart, you're always here.
So, though I mourn your passing on,
I know that love will carry on.
For in the darkness of this grief,
A light still shines, beyond belief.
And though our time together's done,
I know that love has just begun.

So, mourn I will, with all my heart,
But I will not let this tear me apart.
For though you're gone, I'm not alone,
And in my heart, you'll always be home.
Oh, sorrow's grasp, so fierce and cold,
Envelops me in mourning's hold.
But in this embrace, I find release,
And know that love will never cease.

WHISPERS IN THE WIND: A POEM ON LOVE AND LOSS

In the midst of loss, we find our strength,
Amid the darkness, a light at length,
Our hearts may break, our tears may fall,
But we rise above it all.

The pain we feel, a burden to bear,
But within us, a fire to flare,
A will to survive, a spirit to thrive,
To keep moving forward, to keep our dreams alive.

The world may seem confusing and strange,
But we find solace in memories, as they rearrange,
We hold on to the love we shared,
As we move through the stages of despair.

Our grief may be overwhelming,
But we are stronger than we think,
We find strength in the support of others,
And the hope that tomorrow may bring.

Though we may stumble and falter,
We know that we will persevere,
For within us lies a resilience,
That is greater than any fear.

So we mourn our loss, we grieve our pain,
But we find our strength once again,
For in the depths of our sorrow,
We discover a power that we never knew before.

UNBREAKABLE LOVE: A SONG BEYOND DEATH

In death we part, but love endures,
A bond unbroken, steadfast and pure.
Beyond the veil, our souls entwine,
Eternal flames of love divine.

No earthly force can tear apart
The love that beats within our hearts.
Though time may pass and bodies fade,
Our love remains, forever unafraid.

Through storms and trials, we stand strong,
Our love a beacon, a never-ending song.
The stars above may come and go,
But our love burns bright, a constant glow.

Death cannot steal what love has wrought,
The memories we cherish, the battles we fought.
For in our hearts, our love remains,
A flame that burns, a eternal refrain.

So let us hold on, dear and true,
To the love that binds me and you.
For in this life and in the next,
Our love will endure, unfaltering and complex.

ECHOES OF EVERLASTING LOVE: A SONG OF THE UNDYING BOND

In the depths of night,
Amidst the stars so bright,
There lies a love so pure,
That death cannot obscure.

For even as the flesh decays,
And the body fades away,
The love that once did bind,
Will forever be entwined.

Though time may steal our days,
And death may claim our ways,
Our love will never die,
But soar beyond the sky.

For in the realm of the unknown,
Where the winds of fate have blown,
Our love will find a way,
To shine its eternal ray.

So fear not the end that comes,
For our love will overcome,
And in death, we shall be one,
Bound by love that's never done.

For in the end, what we'll find,
Is love that's not confined,
By the limits of this world,
But everlasting and unfurled.

And though our bodies turn to dust,
Our love will forever trust,
That in the vastness of eternity,
Our love will find its destiny.

STRENGTH IN GRIEF: A JOURNEY OF RESILIENCE AND HOPE

In the depths of sorrow's shadowed veil,
When hope seems lost and all seems frail,
A glimmer of strength can yet prevail,
A spark of light in the darkest gale.

For though the heart may weep and ache,
And every breath feels like a break,
There lies within a strength to make,
A path through grief, for one's own sake.

It's not a force that can be sought,
Nor is it sold or cheaply bought,
But something that within is wrought,
From pain and loss and battles fought.

So when the tempest rages strong,
And all that's left seems like a wrong,
Remember, in you lies a song,
Of hope and strength, forever long.

For grief may come and tears may fall,
But in the midst of it all,
There is a power, standing tall,
A strength that's bursty, yet can enthrall.

And though the journey may be tough,
And things may seem too much too rough,
Know that you have enough,
To find the strength, when times are tough.

So take heart and lift your head,
For in you lies a strength instead,
A force that's vast and yet unspread,
A power that will keep you led.

JOURNEY THROUGH MOURNING: FINDING MYSELF IN THE DEPTHS OF SORROW

In the depths of mourning, I search for me,
Lost in a sea of sorrow, where can I be?
My heart shattered, my soul adrift,
I long for a sign, a saving lift.

The world around me is cloaked in grey,
The sun has set on yet another day,
My mind is foggy, my thoughts unclear,
How do I find myself, where do I steer?

I search the corners of my being,
For a glimmer of hope, for some meaning,
But all I find are tears and pain,
And a longing for what can't be reclaimed.

The path ahead seems bleak and long,
My heart heavy with the weight of loss,

But still, I must soldier on,
In search of a new dawn.

For in the depths of sorrow, I see,
A chance to find the real me,
To strip away the masks I wear,
And find the truth that lies beneath the despair.

So I'll journey on, through grief and pain,
With hope in my heart, and faith again,
For though the road ahead is rough,
I know I'll find myself, strong and tough.

And when I do, I'll look back and see,
That mourning was the key,
To unlocking the door of my soul,
And finding the person I was meant to be.

WHEN GRIEF BECOMES A STRENGTH: THE POWER OF RESILIENCE

In the depths of grief, I found a strength
A force that pulsed within me, at length
A burst of power, raw and pure
That helped me face what lay in store

Perplexity consumed my mind
As I searched for meaning, I couldn't find
But within the chaos, I found a light
That guided me through the darkest night

With each passing day, the pain would grow
But so too would my resilience, and so
I faced my sorrow head on, with grace
And found that I could stand in its embrace

For grief, though heavy, need not be a weight
That drags us down, or seals our fate
But rather, it can be a catalyst
That propels us forward, if we persist

So if you find yourself in mourning's hold
Remember that within you lies a bold
And brave spirit, that can weather any storm
And guide you safely to the dawn.

WHISPERS IN THE WIND: REMEMBERING MY GRANDFATHER

In the deep of night, as I lay in my bed,
Thoughts of my grandfather swirl in my head.
A man so strong, so wise and kind,
A pillar of our family left behind.

Tears fall down my cheeks, a torrential rain,
As I try to come to terms with the pain.
The memories flood in, so vivid and clear,
Of times we shared, oh so dear.

We'd sit on his porch, watching the world go by,
And he'd regale me with stories that made me sigh.
Of a life well lived, of struggles and joys,
Of battles fought and victories enjoyed.

But now he's gone, and the world seems so still,
A void in my heart that nothing can fill.
I grieve for him deeply, with all my soul,
And wonder how I'll ever be whole.

But then I remember his words of wisdom,
Of how we must face life's challenges with some optimism.
He may be gone, but his spirit remains,
A legacy of love that forever sustains.

So I'll honor his memory, in all that I do,
With each passing day, I'll strive to renew.
The lessons he taught me, the love he gave,
Will forever be with me, even beyond the grave.

Oh, grandfather, how I miss you so,
But in my heart, your love will forever glow.
I'll keep you close, till we meet again,
In a world beyond this earthly plane.

ECHOES OF LOVE: A POEM OF GRIEF AND REMEMBRANCE FOR MY GRANDMA

In the stillness of the night,
I feel your absence so bright,
Your gentle presence lingers on,
As I grieve for you, my dear grandma, gone.

Your laughter echoes in my mind,
Memories of your love so kind,
The way you held me close and tight,
Now just a bittersweet delight.

The scent of your perfume still lingers,
As I try to hold back the tears,
The pain of losing you so deep,
A wound that refuses to sleep.

The world seems a little less bright,
Without you here, my guiding light,

I try to make sense of it all,
But the confusion just won't stall.

Your absence feels so unreal,
The depth of my loss hard to conceal,
But I'll keep your memory alive,
And cherish the love you always did provide.

In the quiet moments of the day,
I'll remember you in my own way,
And though my heart may ache and yearn,
Your love will forever burn.

So goodbye, dear grandma, for now,
Your memory will always endow,
And though I'll miss you every day,
Your love will never fade away.

FROM DARKNESS TO LIGHT: A POEM OF LOSS AND TRIUMPH

Amidst the void of grief and pain,
I searched for solace, but in vain.
The loss I felt was hard to bear,
A wound so deep, a soul laid bare.

My heart once full of hope and light,
Now shattered by the dark of night.
The road ahead seemed bleak and long,
My spirit weakened, my will not strong.

But as I walked, with heavy feet,
I stumbled upon a hidden treat.
A glimmer of hope, a ray of light,
That showed me there was still a fight.

I picked myself up, and marched ahead,
With a newfound strength, I now led.
I chased my dreams, and faced my fears,
My path was now clear, my vision, clear.

The scars of loss, they still remain,
But they no longer cause me pain.
I've learned to love, to live, to forgive,
And now, I know, I truly live.

So if you're lost, in dark despair,
Remember this, you can repair.
The wounds of loss, they may run deep,
But with time, you too, can rise and leap.

For loss is not the end, my friend,
It's just the start of a new bend.
Embrace the journey, and find your way,
And in the end, you too, will sway.

To the rhythm of life, and all its glory,
A story of loss, and a tale of recovery.

A POETIC JOURNEY OF RESILIENCE

Resilience, the strength to withstand
When life's storms blow us off course and strand
The power to rise again, to stand tall
After we've stumbled, after we've fallen, after we've crawled

It's the voice that whispers, "I can try again"
When failure seems to be the only end
It's the light that shines in the darkest night
The beacon that guides us through the fight

It's the courage to face our fears
To wipe away our sorrowful tears
To take a step, and then another
To keep moving forward, to recover

Resilience is not the absence of pain
It's the ability to endure, to sustain
It's the hope that we carry deep within
The flame that burns, despite the din

It's the journey, not just the destination
The struggle that leads to transformation
It's the beauty that rises from the ashes
The triumph that shines through the clashes

So let us embrace our resilience
Let us cherish its magnificence
For in the end, it is what will remain
Long after the storms have passed, after the pain

UNBREAKABLE FLAME: THE STRENGTH WITHIN

Amidst the chaos and the pain,
The strength within me does remain.
A force unseen, a power untold,
A resilience that never grows old.

My heart has been shattered and torn,
But the fire within me still burns.
I rise up from the ashes of my past,
Stronger than ever, my spirit steadfast.

With each blow, I become more whole,
My inner strength, an unbreakable mold.
Through the trials and the tests,
I stand tall, I am at my best.

Perplexity surrounds me at every turn,
But my inner strength continues to burn.
I push forward with each passing day,
Guided by a force that will not sway.

So bring on the challenges, bring on the strife,
For I know I have the strength to fight.
With each battle, I grow stronger still,
A force to be reckoned with, a force that will.

My burst of power, my unstoppable might,
The strength within me shines so bright.
A beacon of hope, a source of inspiration,
I am a warrior, a force of creation.

So let the world try to bring me down,
For I know that I will stand my ground.
With the strength within me, I will prevail,
A testament to the power of the human will.

UNWAVERING STRENGTH

In the depths of my soul, there lies a power
A strength within that cannot be devoured
It rises up like a flame in the night
Burning bright, casting shadows to take flight

It's a force that defies all logic and reason
A wellspring of power that knows no season
It surges forth with a burst of might
Defying all doubts and fears in sight

This strength within, it perplexes and confounds
With its bursts of energy, it knows no bounds
It comes from a place that is deep and profound
A place where hope and courage are found

It's the voice that whispers "You can do it"
The hand that lifts you up when you feel unfit
It's the light that shines in the darkest hour
Guiding you through with its steadfast power

So when you feel like you're at your end
And you cannot find the strength to ascend

Look within and you will find
The burst of strength to leave all perplexed behind

For the strength within is a force to be reckoned
With its bursts of energy, it cannot be questioned
So harness it well and let it guide your way
For the strength within will never sway.

HOPE'S ETERNAL FLAME

Hope is the fire that burns bright,
In the darkest of nights,
A beacon of light that guides,
Us through the trials of life.

It's the whisper that echoes,
In the chambers of our heart,
A promise of a better tomorrow,
That gives us a brand new start.

Hope is the seed that we sow,
In the barren fields of despair,
Watered with tears and sweat,
It blossoms into a garden fair.

It's the wind that fills our sails,
And carries us across the sea,
A journey full of twists and turns,
But with hope, we'll surely see.

Hope is the song that we sing,
When the world seems to be falling apart,

A melody of faith and love,
That heals the wounds of the heart.

It's the light that shines within,
And brightens up our days,
A ray of hope that never fades,
But forever stays.

So hold on to hope, my friend,
And let it be your guide,
For with hope, all things are possible,
And you can conquer any tide.

SUPPORT

A whisper on the wind, a hand to hold,
A gentle touch when life feels cold,
A listening ear when words won't come,
A light to guide when the day is done.

Support is a bridge that spans the gap,
A refuge from the storm and trap,
A beacon in the darkest night,
A lifeline when we've lost our sight.

It's the comfort of a mother's embrace,
The warmth of a friend's smiling face,
The strength of a lover's steadfast heart,
The grace of a stranger's helping start.

It's the courage to stand up and fight,
The wisdom to see beyond the night,
The faith that keeps us moving on,
The hope that shines when all seems gone.

Support is the thread that weaves us together,
The glue that binds us, now and forever,

The force that lifts us up to the sky,
The magic that makes us feel alive.

So let us cherish every act of support,
And hold it close, with love and rapport,
For in this world of chaos and noise,
Support is the music that fills our joys.

EMBRACING THE DANCE OF CHANGE

Change is the ever-turning wheel of life,
A force that cuts through our struggles and strife,
It tears apart the fabric of our being,
And shakes us to the core of our seeing.

At first, we fight against its unyielding power,
Our minds and hearts struggle in their darkest hour,
But as we surrender to its potent sway,
We find a path towards a brighter day.

The old ways may crumble, the familiar fade,
But new horizons call, and we must not be afraid,
To take the leap and step into the unknown,
To face our fears and let our hearts be shown.

For change is the forge of our souls,
It tempers us with fire and coal,
It breaks us down and builds us anew,
And shapes us into something true.

So let us embrace this dance of change,
And welcome all that may seem strange,
For in its twists and turns we'll find,
The beauty of a life refined.

BELIEVING IN ONESELF

There's a voice inside, that speaks so loud,
It calls you to rise, to stand so proud,
To face the world, and all its might,
And take on challenges, with all your might.

Believing in oneself, is the first step,
To reaching dreams, that others have not kept,
It takes courage and strength, to forge ahead,
And face the challenges, with no shred of dread.

The path may be hard, and full of strife,
But with self-belief, you'll find new life,
A life that's free, from doubt and fear,
A life that's full, of purpose and cheer.

So when the doubts, start to creep in,
And the road ahead, seems far too thin,
Remember the voice, that's deep within,
And believe in yourself, through thick and thin.

For you have the power, to overcome,
And achieve great things, that you've just begun,

Believe in yourself, and you will see,
The world is yours, for eternity.

REACHING OUT: A JOURNEY OF VULNERABILITY AND STRENGTH

In the depths of despair, I cried out for aid,
But my words were lost in the dark and the shade,
I reached for a lifeline, a hand to hold tight,
But my fingers grasped only the emptiness of the night.

The pain within me grew deeper and strong,
I searched for a voice, a comfort, a song,
But the silence echoed, an endless refrain,
Leaving me lost, alone in my pain.

I tried to fight back, to find my own way,
But the weight of my burdens made me sway,
And in my darkest hour, when all seemed lost,
I realized that asking for help was worth the cost.

I opened my heart and let out a scream,
Hoping someone would hear me, and come to my dream,
And though I felt vulnerable, scared and weak,
I knew that reaching out for help was what I seek.

And then, like a beacon, a light in the storm,
A helping hand reached out to keep me warm,
A gentle voice, a kind-hearted soul,
Offered me love, and made me feel whole.

And so, my friend, if you're ever in need,
Don't be afraid to reach out and plead,
For though the journey may be tough and long,
Together, we can make it right and strong.

OVERCOMING LOSS WITH RESILIENCE AND STRENGTH

Amidst the shattered pieces of my life,
I stand with a heart full of strife.
Loss has stripped me of all I knew,
But I'll find my way, I'll start anew.

The road ahead may seem so bleak,
And my tears may flow down my cheek,
But I'll rise from the ashes of my pain,
And dance in the rain once again.

For loss may have taken so much from me,
But it cannot take my will to be free.
I'll pick up the pieces, one by one,
And I'll create a masterpiece, second to none.

My heart may have been broken and bruised,
But with time, it will heal and be infused
With strength, with courage, with love,
And all the things that make life worth dreaming of.

So let the winds of change blow through my life,
And let me embrace this journey without strife.
For I am a warrior, fierce and true,
And I'll conquer this loss, I'll see it through.

WHISPERS OF THE WIND: A JOURNEY OF LOSS AND RESILIENCE THROUGH THE EBB AND FLOW OF LIFE'S TIDES

In the midst of grief and sorrow's wail,
Our hearts are shattered and frail,
Yet in the depths of darkest night,
A glimmer of hope, a flicker of light.

With strength and resilience, we rise,
Through tears and pain, we learn to prize
The memories of those we've lost,
And hold them close, at any cost.

Their absence stings, their voice is still,
But we find comfort in our will
To carry on, to honor their name,
And live our lives, without shame.

The road ahead may be unclear,
With twists and turns, and many a fear,
But we know we'll make it through,
With faith and courage, and love anew.

For every loss, we gain a strength,
That carries us to any length,
And though the scars may never fade,
We rise above, unafraid.

So let us honor those we've lost,
And cherish every moment, at any cost,
For they will always be with us,
In the strength and resilience we thus possess.

UNBREAKABLE SHARDS

In the darkness of despair,
When loss has taken all that's fair,
When tears have flowed and hearts are broken,
And all that's left are words unspoken,
It's easy to feel lost and small,
To wonder if we'll ever stand tall.

But strength is found in the depths of pain,
And hope can rise from the darkest rain.
For every sorrow, there's a tomorrow,
And every ache can lead to growth we borrow.

Resilience is the key to rise,
To spread our wings and reach the skies.
To face the world with courage bold,
And find the light in days of old.

For though we cannot change what's past,
Our future is ours to hold at last.
And though the road may be long and hard,
We have within us an unbreakable shard.

So let us stand with heads held high,
And face the world with a fierce reply.
For though we may have lost today,
Tomorrow is ours to seize and sway.

Let us embrace the strength we've found,
And lift our voices with a mighty sound.
For though we've felt the weight of loss,
Our spirit shines at any cost.

With hope and love we'll carry on,
And find the joy that life has drawn.
For though we've been through depths of pain,
Our strength and resilience shall remain.

THE ROOTS OF STRENGTH

In the depths of grief and sorrow's tide,
Where pain and darkness doth abide,
We find ourselves adrift, alone,
In a world that's lost its joyful tone.

Our hearts are heavy, burdened by the weight
Of loss and longing, of love and fate,
And yet, we stand, though we may sway,
Our spirits strong, our wills to stay.

For though the road ahead is rough,
And tears may fall, and fears may puff,
We know within our very soul,
That strength and hope can make us whole.

And so we rise, with grit and grace,
With steadfast heart and steady pace,
And though our path may wind and weave,
Our faith and courage will not leave.

For in the face of life's great tests,
We find within ourselves our best,

And though we may be bruised and torn,
We rise again, reborn.

So let us hold our heads up high,
And face the world with steely eye,
For though we may be sorely tried,
We shall overcome, with strength and pride.

For in our hearts, we hold the key,
To unlock the door to destiny,
And though we may not know the way,
We trust in hope, and seize the day.

So let us rise, and face the dawn,
With hope and love, and hearts reborn,
And though we may face trials yet,
We will not falter, we will not forget.

For in the end, we shall prevail,
And our spirits, strong and hale,
Shall guide us through life's darkest night,
With strength, hope, and resilience, bright.

THE LIGHT WITHIN

In the midst of darkness, a spark ignites,
A glimmer of hope that illuminates the night.
For loss is a heavy burden to bear,
But strength and resilience will lead us there.

Believe in yourself, for you are strong,
A warrior who will fight against all wrong.
Gather your courage and stand up tall,
For you have the power to conquer all.

The road ahead may be tough and steep,
But never give up, don't you dare to weep.
For hope is a beacon that lights the way,
Leading you through the darkest of days.

Through the valleys of sorrow, you'll climb,
With grit and determination, you'll shine.
With each step you take, you'll gain more power,
And soon you'll overcome, in victory shower.

So don't lose heart, don't give up the fight,
For within you lies a shining light.

A beacon of hope that will never cease,
Guiding you to a place of eternal peace.

And when you reach the end of the road,
With strength and resilience as your code,
You'll look back with pride, and then you'll see,
The person you've become, strong and free.

So go forth, and overcome your loss,
With strength, hope, and resilience as your boss.
Believe in yourself, and you will find,
A new chapter of life, just waiting to unwind.

ETERNAL FLAMES OF LOVE

In life and death, my love will stay,
Forever burning, come what may.
Even when this mortal shell has gone,
Our bond will remain, forever strong.

Death may claim this body of mine,
But not the love that we entwine.
Beyond the veil, we'll still unite,
Our love will glow, an eternal light.

In every moment, in every breath,
Our love will live beyond our death.
The universe will be our canvas,
Our love will be the brush that dances.

For in this life, and in the next,
Our love will never lose its text.
Through all the pain and all the strife,
Our love will be the guiding light.

So let us hold hands and take the leap,
Into the abyss, where secrets keep.

For our love will conquer all,
In life, in death, and beyond the pall.

THE HEALING POWER OF COLLECTIVE GRIEF: FINDING STRENGTH IN COMMUNITY

Amidst the darkness of despair,
When all seems lost, and life unfair,
The power of community shines bright,
A beacon of hope in the darkest night.

We gather together in our pain,
Our tears falling like a heavy rain,
But in this shared grief, we find strength,
And the courage to face life's length.

For though we may feel alone,
Our community has become our home,
A place where we can be vulnerable and true,
Where our wounds are healed by the love we imbue.

The burstiness of our emotions so raw,
In this shared experience, we find a common flaw,
A reminder that life is fragile and fleeting,
But in the warmth of community, we find meaning.

The perplexity of our grief so profound,
In this collective sorrow, we are bound,
Bound by a shared humanity and empathy,
Bound by the power of community.

So let us take solace in each other's embrace,
And find strength in this communal grace,
For in loss, we are not alone,
Together we heal, together we've grown.

NATURE'S EMBRACE: A BALM FOR THE GRIEVING HEART

Amidst the endless hues of green and blue,
Nature spreads her canvas, vibrant and true,
Her gentle touch, a balm to soothe,
The grieving heart, with sorrow imbued.

The rustling leaves, a symphony of peace,
The gentle breeze, a comforting release,
The chirping birds, a melody divine,
Nature's solace, a balm so fine.

The sun-kissed sky, a warm embrace,
The lulling waves, a gentle pace,
The blooming flowers, a gift of grace,
Nature's embrace, a loving space.

The towering mountains, a steadfast friend,
The rushing rivers, a journey without an end,
The starlit sky, a wonder to behold,
Nature's glory, forever untold.

For in nature's arms, we find our rest,
In her beauty, we are forever blessed,
Her mysteries, a source of awe,
Nature's love, forevermore.

So let the grieving heart find solace in her embrace,
In nature's bounty, there's no better place,
For in her presence, we find our way,
And our sorrows, forever held at bay.

NEW BEGINNING: A JOURNEY THROUGH GRIEF AND HEALING

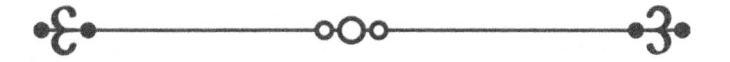

In the darkness of my heart,
A storm is brewing, tearing apart,
The walls that I've built so high,
And now I'm left alone to cry.

The news was sudden, a bolt from the blue,
My heart shattered, what was I to do?
My world crumbled, fell to the ground,
And I was lost, with no way to be found.

The pain was unbearable, a weight on my chest,
I couldn't breathe, couldn't get any rest,
My mind was numb, my body weak,
And all I could do was silently weep.

But slowly, as time passed by,
The storm began to subside,
And in its place, a glimmer of light,
A ray of hope, shining so bright.

With each passing day, I took a step,
Towards healing, towards finding my breath,
And though it hurt, I knew it was right,
To let go of the darkness and embrace the light.

I learnt to smile, to laugh, to love,
To cherish each moment, and rise above,
The pain that once consumed my soul,
Now a distant memory, no longer taking its toll.

And so I stand, stronger than before,
A testament to the journey I bore,
With scars that remind me of what I've been through,
And a heart that's filled with gratitude.

For though the road was rough and steep,
And at times, I felt like I couldn't keep,
Going on, I never lost sight,
Of the hope that guided me through the night.

And now, as I look back at the past,
I see a journey that was meant to last,
A journey of grief, of pain, of healing,
A journey that led me to my new beginning.

CREATIVE HEALING

The human mind is a curious thing,
A vessel for creativity to spring,
When faced with pain or trauma deep,
Our souls must heal and onward leap.

But how to mend a shattered heart?
When every breath feels torn apart?
Through art and craft and passion's fire,
Our spirits rise and we aspire.

With brush and paint, we weave a scene,
Of hope and love and all between,
The canvas holds our pain and grief,
But through it, we find sweet relief.

With pen in hand, we write our tale,
Of triumph and of hardship's trail,
Our words become a healing balm,
As we pour out our hearts in calm.

With notes and chords, we sing a song,
Of sorrow and of joy's headstrong,

Our melody becomes our light,
And guides us through the darkest night.

So let us cherish creativity,
A gift that heals and sets us free,
For in its burst and perplexity,
We find the beauty of our destiny.

THREADS OF MEMORY: WEAVING RESILIENCE IN THE FACE OF LOSS

Memories are the threads that bind us,
Stitching together the moments of our lives,
A tapestry of joy and sorrow,
Of love and loss, of laughter and tears.

They are the touchstones of our past,
The markers of our journey through time,
The anchors that keep us grounded,
When the winds of change blow strong.

For memory is a source of strength,
A reservoir of hope and resilience,
A reminder that we have lived,
And loved, and lost, and survived.

In the face of loss, memory is a balm,
A soothing salve that eases the pain,
A beacon of light that guides us through the darkness,
And a shield that protects us from despair.

For though the present may be bleak,
And the future uncertain and unknown,
Our memories hold the key to our strength,
And the power to help us carry on.

So let us cherish our memories,
And hold them close to our hearts,
For they are the treasures that sustain us,
And the source of our greatest strength and resilience.

GRATEFUL RESILIENCE: THE POWER OF SELF-APPRECIATION IN THE FACE OF LOSS

In the depths of sorrow and despair,
When all seems lost and we can't repair,
Our shattered dreams and broken hearts,
We often forget to play our parts.

Forgetting the beauty in our soul,
And the things that make us whole,
We get lost in the pain and strife,
Ignoring the light that shines in our life.

But if we can learn to appreciate,
The things that make us truly great,
Our inner strength will surely rise,
And we'll find the courage to thrive.

For gratitude is the key,
To unlocking our true destiny,

It's the force that can heal our wounds,
And help us rise above the ruins.

So let us learn to be grateful,
For the blessings that we're able,
To enjoy each and every day,
And the love that comes our way.

For in the face of loss and sorrow,
Gratitude can help us borrow,
Strength and resilience from within,
And find the power to begin again.

LOVE'S HEALING POWER

Love, the great and wondrous force,
A balm for wounds and endless source,
Of strength and hope in darkest hour,
The seed of resilience, healing power.

When loss has left us broken, torn,
And grief consumes us, like a storm,
Love stands firm, a steady hand,
A light that guides us through the sand.

Its touch is gentle, yet so strong,
A melody that heals our song,
It whispers softly to our heart,
And helps us make a brand new start.

For love is not a fleeting thing,
But constant as the birds that sing,
It blossoms forth in every soul,
And makes us feel forever whole.

And though our pain may linger on,
Love helps us find the strength to carry on,

To face each day with courage new,
And see the beauty that is true.

So let us cherish love's sweet grace,
And let it be our resting place,
For in its light we'll find the way,
To heal and thrive another day.

UNVEILING THE POWER OF SELF-CARE: A JOURNEY TOWARDS RESILIENCE AND HEALING

In the midst of grief and pain,
Our spirits may feel bound in chains.
But there's a truth we must embrace,
Self-care is key in this race.

When loss has left us feeling weak,
It's tempting to shut down and retreat.
But self-care can be our shield,
To protect us from wounds unhealed.

It's not just bubble baths and wine,
Though those can be quite divine.
Self-care is a mindset too,
Of loving and being kind to you.

It's the courage to face your fears,
To process all your painful tears.

It's the discipline to prioritize,
Your health and wellness, no compromise.

It's the willingness to seek support,
To find the help that you've been taught.
It's the strength to ask for what you need,
To honor your grief and let it lead.

So take care of yourself, my friend,
It's a journey without an end.
But know that with each step you take,
Resilience grows, and strength awakes.

FINDING LIGHT IN THE DARK: THE HEALING POWER OF LAUGHTER

Laughter echoes through the halls of grief,
A tonic for the soul that brings relief,
When tears have fallen and the heart is heavy,
Humor can work wonders, keeping us steady.

Through trials and troubles, it's easy to feel down,
To sink into sorrow and wear a permanent frown,
But laughter can cut through the clouds of despair,
Making the world a little brighter, a little less unfair.

It's a funny thing, this humor we share,
A little bit of levity, a reminder we care,
It's a reminder that life is worth living,
That joy can still be found, despite the suffering.

For when we laugh, we feel a little lighter,
A little more free, a little bit brighter,
And in that moment, we find a bit of peace,
A respite from the pain, a moment's release.

So let us laugh, in the face of our sorrow,
For in that laughter, we'll find a brighter tomorrow,
We'll build our resilience, and we'll find our way,
Through humor and hope, to a brighter day.

LEGACY: THE EVERLASTING LIGHT

In the depths of sorrow, we may find
A source of strength, not left behind
For though our loved ones may be gone
Their legacy endures, and we carry on

Their laughter echoes in our hearts
Their kindness guides us through the dark
Their wisdom lingers, ever near
Their love sustains us, year after year

Through trials and pain, we may falter
But their memory remains, a steady altar
A beacon of hope, a ray of light
Their legacy inspires us to fight

To honor their legacy, we rise
To embrace the world with open eyes
To live our lives with purpose true
For in doing so, we honor you

Though the road ahead may be steep
We carry their memory, forever to keep
Their legacy, a source of power
A guiding force, in life's darkest hour

So let us find solace in their embrace
And let their legacy shine on our face
For though they may be gone from sight
Their legacy lives on, in us tonight.

THE ART OF LETTING GO

In the depths of sorrow and pain,
When life has dealt its cruellest blow,
We often seek someone to blame,
And our anger and hurt continue to grow.

But the path to healing is forgiveness,
A power that can set us free,
It may not come easy, I confess,
But it's the key to building resilience, you'll see.

For when we forgive, we let go,
Of the bitterness and the rage,
And we open our hearts to hope,
To a brighter and more peaceful stage.

We release the burden of hurt,
And we embrace the light of love,
We find the strength to move forward,
To rise above.

Forgiveness is not a sign of weakness,
But a symbol of our inner strength,

It takes courage to let go of our distress,
And to embrace a new beginning at length.

So, let us forgive and let us heal,
Let us rebuild what was torn apart,
Let us find solace in what we feel,
And let forgiveness be the start.

For it is through forgiveness that we find,
The resilience to endure,
To weather the storms and bind,
The wounds that we once thought too obscure.

And so, I urge you to forgive,
To let go of the pain and strife,
For in forgiveness, we can truly live,
And find the courage to thrive.

FINDING STRENGTH IN MUSIC'S EMBRACE

In every note and melody, a story unfolds,
A tale of pain and triumph, of joys and woes.
The beat, the rhythm, and the harmony,
Can mend broken hearts and heal misery.

When grief weighs heavy on the soul,
And tears flow like a ceaseless stream,
Music can be the balm that consoles,
A refuge that brings hope and a dream.

With every strum of the guitar,
And every beat of the drum,
The pain eases, the heart beats calm,
And the spirit begins to overcome.

For in the power of music lies,
The resilience to rise above the pain,
To find the strength to carry on,
And embrace life once again.

So let the music take hold of you,
And fill you with its magic and wonder,
For in its embrace, you'll find the clue,
To overcome the storms and thunder.

Let the music be your guide,
Through the darkest of days,
And with its help, you'll surely find,
The light that shines through the haze.

For music is the language of the heart,
The key to unlocking the soul,
And in its power, we find the art,
Of healing, of hope, and of making us whole.

THE TRANSFORMATIVE POWER OF TRAVEL

Amidst the pain of loss and grief,
Travel can offer much relief.
A journey to a distant land,
Can help us heal and understand.

The world's a wondrous, vast expanse,
With beauty, love, and happenstance.
Through travel, we can find our way,
To hope and strength on every day.

The burstiness of new terrain,
Can free our minds from endless pain.
Perplexity of sights unseen,
Can spark a fire, a flame so keen.

From mountaintops to oceans blue,
Travel can make us feel brand new.
With each new step we take, we find,
A fresh perspective on the mind.

So if you're lost in sorrow's grip,
Pack your bags, take that one trip.
Through travel, you will find a way,
To heal, to cope, and seize the day.

THE TRANSFORMATIVE POWER OF PETS IN TIMES OF SORROW AND HEALING

The wag of a tail, the purr of a cat,
The warmth of their fur, the weight of their pat,
Pets have a power, a magic all their own,
To lift us up, to help us find our way home.

They comfort us in times of sorrow,
Loyal companions, today and tomorrow,
A constant presence in a world that's changing,
Their love for us, unconditionally reigning.

They greet us at the door, with a smile on their face,
Ready to love us, and offer their embrace,
Their little quirks, and their funny ways,
Bring joy to our hearts, and brighten our days.

In the midst of our pain, they sit by our side,
And remind us of the love that's still alive,
Their presence a comfort, in the dark of the night,
A source of resilience, a guiding light.

For pets have a way, of helping us to heal,
To find our strength, and start to feel,
A little bit of hope, a little bit of peace,
A little bit of comfort, as our grief starts to ease.

So let us cherish, these furry friends,
Who stand by us, until the very end,
For in their love, we'll find our way,
Through the darkest of nights, and the hardest of days.

TRADITIONS, THE KEEPERS OF HOPE

Amidst the chaos and the pain,
When nothing else can ease the strain,
Our traditions and our rituals remain,
A source of comfort, steadfast and sane.

The loss we feel can overwhelm,
A storm that rages, a sea that's helm,
But our customs, they're like a realm,
A refuge where we can take the helm.

From lighting candles to saying prayers,
From laying wreaths to shedding tears,
Our traditions give us strength and bears,
A solace that can last for years.

The memories we keep alive,
Of loved ones who did not survive,
The rituals that we still revive,
A thread that helps us to survive.

For though our hearts may break in two,
Our traditions see us through,
A light that shines, a path to pursue,
And give us hope for a better view.

So let us honor those we've lost,
And cherish all the things they've cost,
For our traditions, they're the host,
That keep us safe and never lost.

BONDS OF FRIENDSHIP

In times of grief, when life feels bleak,
It's often friendship that we seek.
A shoulder to cry on, an ear to hear,
A kindred soul to hold us near.

The bond of friends can be so strong,
A lifeline when we feel alone.
Through tears and laughter, highs and lows,
They're there for us, our rock, our foes.

Their support can give us wings to fly,
To face the world, to try and try.
Their love can give us hope and light,
To see beyond the darkest night.

With every hug, with every smile,
We find the strength to go the mile.
With every word, with every touch,
We find the courage to be enough.

So let us cherish those we hold dear,
Our friends, our confidants, so near.

For in their presence, we find our way,
Through life's burstiness and perplexity, day by day.

FINDING STRENGTH IN HELPING OTHERS

Amidst the trials of life, we find our way
Through heartache, grief, and pain each day
But in the depths of sorrow's night
We find that helping others can give us light

For when we lend a hand to those in need
We plant a seed of hope and strength indeed
And though we may be broken and frail
Our kindness can make the hardest heart prevail

In loss and tragedy, we may feel alone
But helping others can become our throne
A source of resilience, a wellspring of might
That keeps us shining in the darkest of night

The perplexity of life's mysterious ways
Can leave us wondering, lost in a daze
But when we offer love and care to another
We find a burst of joy that cannot be smothered

So let us embrace the power of giving
And find in it the strength for living
For in helping others, we find our way
Through the darkest of nights to a brighter day.

THE HEALING POWER OF FOOD

Food, the healer of souls,
A balm for the heart that aches,
A tool for building resilience,
When grief, our spirit breaks.

The sizzle of onions in a pan,
The aroma of spices in the air,
A simmering pot of soup or stew,
Comfort food, beyond compare.

For when the world seems too much,
And we feel alone in our sorrow,
A plate of food can bring us back,
To a brighter tomorrow.

With every bite we take,
We can nourish both body and mind,
A simple act of self-care,
To help us leave our pain behind.

From a bowl of warm oatmeal,
To a bowl of hearty chili,
Food can bring us comfort,
And help us find our way, still.

So let us savor every bite,
And let our hearts be filled,
For with each nourishing meal we take,
Our resilience is surely built.

PENNING STRENGTH: HEALING THROUGH WRITING

Ink spills onto paper like tears on a face
As words flow from a soul that's lost its place
Yet through the sorrow and the pain we find
That writing is a balm to ease the mind

The page becomes a canvas for our pain
A place to pour our heartache like rain
We paint our stories with each pen stroke
And find in writing, a way to cope

Weaving tales of love and loss and hope
Our words take flight and help us to cope
With every sentence, every rhyme we write
We build resilience and strength to fight

Through metaphors and imagery we find
A way to heal the scars left behind
The pen becomes a sword to battle grief
As we write our way to sweet relief

The power of words can be immense
A force to help us break down the fence
That separates us from the world we knew
And opens up a path to start anew

So let us write with fervor and with grace
Let our words become a sacred space
To honor all that we have lost and gained
And build resilience through our pain.

ART'S COMFORT: A SOURCE OF SOLACE IN THE NIGHT

Amidst the darkness and the pain,
When all seems lost and hope in vain,
Art can be a guiding light,
A source of solace in the night.

Like a gentle breeze on troubled sea,
A soothing balm for the wounded me,
Art can heal the heart that's broken,
And bring the words that remain unspoken.

In a painting, there's a world unseen,
A place of beauty, of love serene,
Where colors blend in perfect grace,
And sadness fades without a trace.

In a melody, there's a voice that sings,
Of memories lost and forgotten things,
Of love that lingers, of dreams that stay,
And hopes that guide us on our way.

In a poem, there's a truth that lies,
In every word, in every line,
Of life's struggles, of its joys and tears,
And the strength that comes with facing fears.

So let us turn to art in times of need,
And find in it the strength to lead,
A life of beauty, of hope and grace,
In the midst of loss, in every place.

OVERCOMING GRIEF WITH THE SUPPORT OF FAMILY

In the depths of grief, I found my soul adrift
Lost in a sea of sorrow and despair
But in the storm of emotions that did lift
I found my family, who did fiercely care

My mother, a tree rooted deep and strong
Her branches stretched out to shield and protect
Her love, a comforting lullaby song
That soothed my heart with each note effect

My father, a rock in the raging waves
His steadfastness a constant guide
His wisdom, a light that forever paves
A path through the darkness, a beacon to abide

My sister, a phoenix born from ash
Her spirit rising with each passing day
Her courage, a flame that did not falter or crash
A symbol of hope that did not sway

Together, they formed a fortress of love
A place of refuge in the midst of the storm
Their unwavering support like wings of a dove
That carried me through the grief and kept me warm

In their embrace, I found strength and resilience
Their love a balm that healed my broken heart
And though the pain of loss may never truly silence
Their presence is a comfort that shall never depart

For in the story of my grief and loss
It is the story of family's love that shall be told
A tale of strength and resilience, despite the cost
A story of a family that is priceless and gold.

RESILIENCE IN MOTION: THE HEALING POWER OF SPORTS AND PHYSICAL ACTIVITY

With every stride and every leap,
The body and soul in harmony keep,
Through sweat and toil, we find our strength,
And learn to persevere at length.

In sports, we find a refuge true,
A place to heal and start anew,
For when our hearts are heavy with grief,
It is through movement, we find relief.

We run to leave our troubles behind,
Our feet pounding the pavement, in time,
And as we push through each and every mile,
Our worries fade, and we begin to smile.

With each swing of the racket, we release,
The anger and pain that we can't appease,

And with each serve, we let go of our fear,
Knowing that we have the power to persevere.

In the pool, we feel the weight of our sorrow,
Washed away with every stroke we follow,
As we glide through the water with grace,
Our troubles seem to disappear without a trace.

On the field, we feel alive,
As we fight to keep our hopes alive,
Our bodies and minds in unison,
As we strive to reach our vision.

In sports, we find a way to cope,
To build resilience, and learn to hope,
And through the sweat and tears, we find,
That strength and courage, are all in our mind.

So take a step, and take a chance,
Embrace the power of sports, and dance,
With each breath, and every move,
You'll find the strength, to conquer and prove.

SERENITY'S TRIUMPH: HOW MEDITATION EMPOWERS RESILIENCE AND HEALS GRIEF

In the midst of pain and sorrow,
When the world seems bleak and hollow,
Meditation is the key,
To help you cope and set you free.

With eyes closed and breath held deep,
Your mind will slowly start to leap,
Into a realm of peace and calm,
Where grief no longer holds its charm.

As you sit in stillness and silence,
Your heart will find its own balance,
And every thought that once brought pain,
Will slowly begin to wane.

Like a flower that blooms in the rain,
Your spirit will rise once again,

With renewed strength and resilience,
And a sense of calm and brilliance.

As you meditate day by day,
The shadows of grief will fade away,
And the light of hope will shine through,
As you discover a strength within you.

So take a deep breath and let it go,
And let your heart and mind both flow,
Into a world of peace and love,
That surrounds you like a gentle dove.

For meditation is the key,
To help you cope and set you free,
From the chains of grief and pain,
And to find your joy once again.

THE COMFORT OF ADVENTURE

In the wake of loss, we often feel adrift
Aimlessly wandering through life's shifts
But in adventure lies a comforting gift
A balm to the soul that can give us a lift

The world is a canvas, waiting to be painted
With colors and textures that leave us elated
In the face of loss, it's easy to feel jaded
But the unknown can bring us a joy unaided

Take to the sea, and let the waves carry you
To faraway lands, where dreams come true
The salty air, the endless blue
Can heal the wounds that cut us through

Or climb a mountain, with the wind in your hair
The challenge may seem steep, but the view is rare
The summit may be elusive, but the journey is fair
And the strength it brings, a comfort to bear

Adventure can be a balm, a source of solace
In the face of loss, it can be a palace
Of memories and experiences, that we can harness
To keep us going, when life is the darkest

So take a leap of faith, and chase your dreams
The world is waiting, bursting at the seams
With wonders and magic, that can reignite your beams
And give you the resilience, to face life's extremes.

THE HEALING POWER OF KINDNESS

Amidst the chaos and pain,
Kindness shines like a ray of light,
A balm for wounds that leave a stain,
A salve that soothes with all its might.

When grief strikes with its brutal force,
And shatters our world to pieces,
Kindness becomes a healing source,
That helps us find our inner creases.

Like a gentle breeze on a summer's day,
Kindness whispers words of comfort,
It wipes our tears and shows the way,
To a brighter tomorrow that we can consort.

It's like a warm blanket on a cold winter's night,
That wraps us in its gentle embrace,
It tells us that everything will be alright,
And helps us find our inner grace.

Kindness is like a river that flows,
Through the valleys and over the hills,
It brings life to everything it touches,
And fills us with hope that heals.

In moments of darkness and despair,
Kindness can be our saving grace,
It lifts us up when we feel bare,
And helps us find a brighter place.

So let us be kind to one another,
And use this powerful tool,
To build resilience and recover,
From the wounds that make us feel dull.

For kindness is a force to be reckoned with,
A beacon that shines in the darkest night,
It helps us cope and helps us live,
And makes our world a little more bright.

THE GUIDING LIGHT OF EDUCATION

In the depths of sorrow and despair,
When loss and pain seem all too fair,
Education can be a guiding light,
A source of comfort in the darkest night.

Like a tree that bends in the wind,
Yet stands tall when the storm rescinds,
Education too can teach us to flex,
To adapt and withstand life's cruel effects.

It's a candle that burns bright,
Even in the midst of the bleakest night,
A beacon that guides us through the mist,
A steady hand that we can't resist.

Through books and lectures, we find solace,
In knowledge, we discover a new promise,
Of a world beyond our grief and pain,
Where hope and joy can still remain.

Education is a balm for the soul,
A healer that makes us feel whole,
In the face of loss, it helps us to cope,
A ray of sunshine, a symbol of hope.

So let us embrace the power of learning,
And in its embrace find our yearning,
For a life that's rich and full of grace,
Where comfort and resilience always have a place.

THE MAGIC OF ACCEPTANCE

Amidst the tumultuous tides of life
When loss and sorrow cut like a knife
It's easy to be consumed by despair
And let hopelessness linger in the air

But in the depths of our darkest days
There's a powerful force that can light the way
It's the magic of acceptance, that rare gem
That can bring us comfort, and help us stem

The overwhelming flood of grief and pain
And allow us to find peace again

Like a warm blanket on a cold winter night
Or a ray of sun breaking through the clouds in flight
Acceptance is a balm for the soul
That can help us find our way back to whole

It's the gentle hand that guides us through
The stormy seas of loss and rue
And helps us see that life goes on
Even when we feel like we can't be strong

Acceptance is the light in the dark
That can ignite a fire in our heart
And give us the strength to carry on
When all seems lost and hope is gone

So let us embrace the power of acceptance
And find solace in its loving presence
For it's a source of comfort and resilience
That can help us weather any circumstance.

PIXELS OF SOLACE: TECHNOLOGY'S ROLE IN HEALING THE HEART

Amidst the shroud of sorrow and despair,
When life seems like a burden hard to bear,
We turn to technology, our trusty friend,
Whose aid we seek till the bitter end.

The glowing screen, our portal of hope,
A refuge for the heart, a salve for the soul,
We reach out to the world, and it reaches back,
An infinite web of love, never to lack.

In times of loss, we seek solace online,
To share our stories, to seek a sign,
To find a community of kindred hearts,
Who understand our pain, and play their part.

We post our memories, our pictures, our fears,
And find in the pixels, a source of tears,
We find in the memes, a reason to smile,
A glimmer of hope, in this life so fragile.

Technology is our bridge to the beyond,
A conduit to the ones who've gone,
A digital legacy, a virtual shrine,
Where their memory lives, forever divine.

We may lose our loved ones, but not their essence,
For in the digital world, they find a presence,
A source of comfort, a source of strength,
To carry on, to go the length.

So let us embrace this new frontier,
And let technology be our comfort near,
For in its embrace, we find a way,
To heal our hearts, and face each day.

ACTIVISM'S FLAME

Amidst the chaos and the strife,
In times of loss and pain,
When darkness seems to claim our life,
And hope seems all in vain.

Activism can be a light,
A beacon shining bright and true,
A way to channel all our might,
And do what we must do.

It's like a river flowing strong,
Rushing over rocks and stones,
A force that carries us along,
And helps us find our way home.

It's like a tree that stands so tall,
And reaches up towards the sky,
A symbol of our strength and all,
That we can never die.

It's like a flame that burns so bright,
A fire that never fades,

A spark that ignites our might,
And never leaves us in the shades.

For activism is not just a cause,
But a source of hope and peace,
A way to rise above the flaws,
And make our pain decrease.

So let us raise our voices high,
And stand up for what we believe,
For even when we face goodbye,
Our activism won't leave.

And though we may be hurt and broken,
Our spirits will still rise,
For through activism, we've awoken,
And found our way to the skies.

THE HEALING POWER OF COOKING

In the kitchen she stands, lost in thought,
With memories of her grandmother she sought.
Her heart still aching from the loss,
Her soul longing for her grandmother's close.

But here in the kitchen, her spirit is eased,
As she cooks her grandmother's signature recipes.
The familiar scents and tastes she savors,
Bringing back memories of their time together.

A pinch of salt, a dash of love,
She remembers how her grandmother would approve.
With each dish she prepares with care,
She feels her grandmother's presence there.

Through the tears and the pain,
The kitchen becomes her refuge again.
As she channels her grief into each meal,
She finds comfort in the familiarity and feels.

For even though her grandmother is gone,
Her love and memory forever live on.
And with each meal that she cooks and bakes,
Her grandmother's spirit she celebrates.

ACKNOWLEDGMENTS:

I would like to begin by expressing my deepest gratitude to those who have supported me on this journey. To my family, who have always been my biggest fans and who have provided endless love and encouragement throughout my life. To my friends, who have been a constant source of inspiration, support, and laughter.

To my readers, who have embraced my work with open hearts and minds. Your feedback, encouragement, and enthusiasm have meant the world to me.

I would also like to express my gratitude to the poets who have come before me and who have inspired me with their work. Your words have shown me the power of language to heal, to uplift, and to transform.

To everyone who has played a role in the creation of this book, I extend my deepest thanks and appreciation. May these poems offer comfort, solace, and hope to those who are facing loss, and may they remind us all of the beauty and resilience that lies within us.

If you found inspiration, comfort, or solace in this book, please consider taking a moment to share your thoughts and leave a review on the platform where you purchased it, or on popular book review websites. Your feedback would mean the world to me and help spread the power of these poems to others who may benefit from them. Thank you for your support.

SUPPORT SERVICES

Grief can be a difficult journey, but you don't have to face it alone. If you have been touched by any of the topics in this book, it may be beneficial to reach out to those closest to you for support, or to consider the many resources available to help you navigate the grieving process.

1. Friends and family: Share your feelings with those you trust, and don't hesitate to lean on their support. Sometimes, just talking to someone who knows and cares about you can help you through tough times.
2. Support groups: Many local communities, hospitals, and non-profit organisations offer support groups for individuals who are experiencing grief. These groups can provide a safe space to share your experiences and connect with others who are going through similar situations.
3. Professional counselling: A therapist or counsellor who specialises in grief and loss can provide valuable guidance and support. They can help you process your emotions, develop coping strategies, and work towards healing.
4. Spiritual or religious support: If you have a spiritual or religious background, consider reaching out to a faith leader or attending services or gatherings. Many people find solace in their beliefs during difficult times.

5. Self-care: Taking care of your physical, emotional, and mental well-being is essential during the grieving process. This can include activities such as exercise, healthy eating, meditation, and making time for hobbies or relaxation.

6. Hotlines and helplines: If you're feeling overwhelmed and need immediate support, consider reaching out to a crisis hotline or helpline. These confidential services provide trained volunteers who are available to listen, offer emotional support, and provide referrals to local resources.

Remember that there is no right or wrong way to grieve, and everyone's journey is different. It may take time, but healing is possible with the right support and resources. Don't hesitate to seek help if you need it and be patient with yourself as you navigate this challenging experience.

Printed in Great Britain
by Amazon